To Christine.

Happy Easter Hols.   1993.

All his Love.
John
xxx

Great VS Climbs
in the Lake District

Great VS Climbs
in the Lake District

TIM NOBLE

C·O·N·T·E·N·T·S

British Library Cataloguing in Publication Data

Noble, Tim, 1950–
  Great VS climbs in the Lake District.
  1. Cumbria. Lake District. Rock climbing. – Manuals
  I. Title
  796.5′223′094278

ISBN 0-7153-9247-6
Text and uncredited photographs © Tim Noble 1989

Typeset by Typesetters (Birmingham) Ltd
Smethwick, West Midlands
and printed in Portugal by Resopal
for David & Charles Publishers plc
Brunel House   Newton Abbot   Devon
Colour origination by Regent Publishing Services, Hong Kong

I·N·T·R·O·D·U·C·T·I·O·N

A hundred years ago only a handful of men climbed in Lakeland regularly, and then on very few cliffs. Today, on a bank holiday, many thousands of men and women will be climbing on Lakeland crags, and doing climbs that their predecessors would never have believed possible. Such has been the rate of development of the sport that in the Lake District at least, it now seems that every significant piece of rock has had its obvious lines climbed. Given the number of active climbers operating regularly in the Lakes and elsewhere in Britain, this is not surprising. Nor is it surprising when one considers that out of the approximately 23 million hectares that constitute this country's land forms, only 10ha are Cumbrian cliffs. There is little new left to discover, it seems.

For the middle-grade climber, these observations may be of no importance; she or he will continue to seek out those routes that remain the classics of their grade and continue to visit those cliffs they know best. Despite the fact that the Lake District is a very small area and most crags can be reached from a road inside two hours, many climbers still tend to base themselves in one valley for a holiday period and climb exclusively on crags in that valley. The paradox is that, despite our cars, we often seem more conservative and parochial in our choice of climb than were our ancestors. We may also be slightly less adventurous, preferring the company of several other noisy teams on a roadside crag to the windy solitude of a high coombe. Some crags attract more attention than others, of course, but it is odd that in such a small mountain area some valleys remain deserted while others are uncomfortably crowded. Crags, too, come in and out of fashion. It is rare for Kern Knotts to be busy these days; but it is a widely known fact that many of the best middle-grade rock climbs in the Lake District are to be found only by a walk of an hour or more. Now some modern climbers might turn their noses up at walking for an hour or more to climb a 200ft (61m) VS climb, preferring to spend the time on a roadside crag attempting the same extremely difficult climb, perhaps. But our predecessors thought otherwise. For them, the walk to and from a high mountain crag was integral to the experience of the day, not something separate, to be endured before the real experience of the rock could be enjoyed.

The author high on North West Arête. Gimmer Crag (Sally Noble)

Men like Lehmann J. Oppenheimer, writing of the delights of climbing in the late 1890s, could get quite strident about this topic:

I have no sympathy with the ever-increasing number who look on the tramp to the foot of the crags as a 'beastly grind.' It will be disastrous to the sport of climbing if its devotees cease to love the mountains as a whole, as the older men did, and wish only for crags.

Prophetic words indeed. But it was by no means only the Victorians who enjoyed their walking as much as their climbing. Archer Thompson, writing about the 'modern' generation of climber associated with H. M. Kelly, recorded what was common in his day:

The modern climber will perhaps ascend Helm Crag, then descend into Far Easedale, climb Deer Bield Crag Gully, go on to Pavey Ark, ascend Big Gully, descend Little Gully, ascend Rake End Chimney and then after a climb or two on Kern Knotts end up at Wasdale Head. They are like that nowadays.

Although the routes Thompson was talking about are easy by modern standards, many climbers would still be pushed to emulate this sort of achievement today, even if they thought it worth the effort. Nor is it so long ago that the habit of combining climbs with walks became unfashionable. Peter Harding, a contemporary of Dolphin, Peascod and Birkett, but climbing almost exclusively in Wales and the Peak, was once criticised for climbing to the exclusion of walking:

On returning [to Helyg] late that evening Harding and Dyke announced that they had been over Tryfan, Glyder Fach, down to the Pass and back over Glyder Fawr. 'Very good,' was the reply, 'but you have taken rather a long time over it – a good walker would have been back in four hours.' They had in fact done thirty climbs up and sometimes down . . .

And Dolphin himself would think nothing of combining climbs on Esk Buttress with climbs in Langdale in one day. So why is it so unfashionable today?

This book is intended for those rock climbers who, like me, enjoy climbing at the Very Severe grade and who still get excited about combining their climbing with long mountain walks. The aim of the book is to offer the keen mountaineer a personal evocation of twenty-seven of the finest Lakeland VS climbs which are linked by circular walks to form ten taxing mountain expeditions.

(left) *Will Randle trying to avoid the holly on the abseil of Miner's Girdle*

(overleaf) *the author on the way to Pillar on the Robinson Cairn path* (Terry Gifford)

The climbs are all at the VS grade because I believe that is still the grade that many casual climbers feel offers them challenge and which can be attempted in marginal conditions (an important consideration in the Lakes), or when wearing boots and carrying a sack. Many of these selected VS climbs were put up between the war years by the best climbers of their generation and in many cases they form not only the most obvious if not the classic lines of the crags, but also they are often milestones in the development of the sport. To attempt Engineer's Slabs on Gable Crag, for instance, in poor conditions after climbing Kern Knotts Crack and Eagle's Nest Ridge Direct is to get a unique insight into the history of the sport and the strengths of our predecessors. Such insights are important if we want to weigh up the achievements of our contemporaries.

Climbs were chosen to fit the walks and for their intrinsic worth, and although many of these round walks may seem artificial or contrived, I have found that my enjoyment of the climbing has been heightened by walking round the crags rather than driving scores of miles from one crag and valley to another. The long walks linking the crags have helped me to appreciate the moun-tains more and learn more about my companions in extended conversations while we have walked.

The maps which accompany the text are not intended to be definitive; they should be used, as should the walking notes, with the appropriate Ordnance Survey sheets in the new Outdoor Leisure series 1:25,000. Similarly, readers will want to consult the appropriate climbing guide-books (always mentioned in the text) since my writing, though faithful to the climb, will not be the same as pitch descriptions.

This publication is not intended to record a feat or set a challenge – so many climbs in so many hours or days. But a fit team with judiciously placed camp-sites and two cars might manage the climbs comfortably in eight or nine days. For myself, ten days have proved more amenable, and I imagine climbers with young families may find the same.

Finally, I should perhaps say a word about erosion and conservation. At the outset of the project, I was concerned that, by drawing people's attention again to selected climbs – some of which are popular and acknowledged classics, often spoken or written about – I was contributing to the process of cliff overkill that books like *Hard Rock* and *Classic Rock* have been accused by some of fostering. That concern has never completely disappeared; but I have come to realise that few people are now climbing many of these routes. This is partly because of the generally poor weather conditions and partly because of the length of the walks to the crags. While Haste Not, on White Ghyll, will always be a popular climb (and beginning now to show signs of serious wear and tear),

Walking to Buckstone Howe, Buttermere, a sliver of light in the distance (John Baker)

a route like Beowulf on Scrubby Crag will probably never get the same sort of constant use. But it is obvious that climbers need to widen their horizons if some great climbs are not to be irreparably damaged while others disappear through neglect. There is much still to be rediscovered about Lakeland crags, and by VS climbers. I can only say in my defence that on many days my partners and I were alone on major crags during public holidays. Sometimes, indeed, I have suspected that on returning to a route after a month or more to try again for a photograph, the route has not had an ascent in the interim. If we approach these climbs (like all other climbs), bearing in mind one of the recommendations of the 1984 Brockhole Conference (reiterated at the Charlotte Mason College conference on Adventure and Environmental Awareness in 1987), then we may, at the very least, be aware of our present responsibilities for the care of our environment and the pressing need to conserve this beautiful mountain area for the climbers and walkers of the future.

The human being is a part of, and not superior to nature, and therefore needs to approach nature in all aspects with awareness and some humility. All those who use the outdoors should take care to minimise disturbance of all other life and natural forms.

1 L·A·N·G·D·A·L·E

The Walk from New Dungeon Ghyll to White Ghyll

From Lake Windermere the Langdale Pikes have the shape of mountains but the look of hills. This is an illusion. Langdale is so easy of access that generations of would-be walkers and mountaineers have been lured by this optical trick to the New Dungeon Ghyll car park. But from here the Pikes are different: open fell-sides of rough scree and tussocky grass rear above the tarmac. Most walkers will make an effort and toil up the newly created Stickle Ghyll path to the dam, but no further. Others, however, will want more exciting challenges – on the Langdale round, perhaps, or over Bowfell to the hub of Lakeland at Esk Hause. But this day's outing combines three of Langdale's most popular peaks with 650ft (183m) of rock climbing and a circular walk of some 4 miles (6km) to provide the keen mountaineer with a challenge.

An early start is recommended so that you start climbing on White Ghyll in the cool morning and finish on Raven Crag in late afternoon shadows. Apart from the rough scree at the top of White Ghyll and the bottom of the Middle Fell path, the ground is straightforward. Track shoes should be adequate.

On the path which leads past the hotel as if to ascend Stickle Ghyll, a signpost points to an early crossing of the ghyll via a bridge on the right. This leads to another carefully rebuilt path and then, almost immediately, a muddy track (signposted White Ghyll) going eastwards, behind a wall, almost back down the dale. This path finishes at the dried bed of a stream – White Ghyll. Turn up the stream bed and follow a rough path on its (true) left bank. Approximately 200ft (61m) above an obvious sycamore, in the ghyll bed, is a large, flat boulder. The start of the first climb of the day, Haste Not, is exactly opposite.

KNOTS

Haste Not (4b, 4c, 4b), White Ghyll Crag (J. Birkett and L. Muscroft, May 1948)

I do not experience your experience
But I experience you as experiencing.
I experience myself as experienced by you

(*The Politics of Experience*, R. D. Laing)

Blea Rigg sits in middle Langdale like a big green gumshield, protecting Rydal Water below its eastern lee slopes from the heavy-punching south-westerlies that crash down Oxendale. Sometimes, when the winds come from the north and west, over Rossett Gill, the Rigg acts like the volute of a turbine accelerating the air and turning it into vicious whirlpools of black energy. Climbing on White Ghyll Crag in these conditions can be trying because the crag lies high up on the Rigg in a gully, open to the drumming wind.

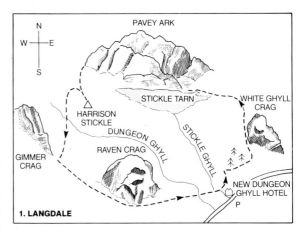

1. LANGDALE

From the New Dungeon Ghyll car park the cliff is obvious, seemingly a continuation of the friendly outcrop of Scout Crag. It looks as loose, cracked and broken as an old molar. But appearances are deceptive. Its high-angle slabs capped by overhangs provide some of the most

The author belaying Will Randle on the crux of Haste Not (Ian Smith)

exposed and exciting middle-grade climbing in Langdale, and certainly one of the best short VS climbs in England, Haste Not.

On the September Saturday that John and I set off to climb, laden down with camping gear as well as ropes, a light drizzle was tickling at our cuffs and necks, but there was little water in the ghyll. So full of broken boulders and vegetation is it in its lower reaches that it very rarely rushes white. In droughts, however, it becomes a hot red scar, and you have to kneel to hear the cool noise of the trickling stream deep below the stones. But after several days of heavy rain the ghyll flashes briefly again on the hillside.

White Ghyll Crag from the New Dungeon Ghyll car park (Ian Smith)

Although it was now raining steadily, other teams were starting to climb. We recognised a strong contingent of the Klingon Climbing Club from Bath, down our way, strung out on White Ghyll Wall and Gordian Knot. They were calling to one another and their base-support team for guide-book guidance. It was time to climb. John looked slyly at me and proceeded to uncoil the ropes with my ends upper-most; he obviously wanted the exciting second pitch that was also dry. I racked the nuts reluctantly. The rain was dispiriting. I looked at John and wondered if he really wanted to climb. Where were those small behavioural clues, those tell-tale gestures and movements we all learn from our regular climbing partners that show something of their inner feelings or moods? It might be a nervous rechecking of the guide, or the way the boots are laced up for instance, but John was happily finding a belay beside the soggy slab, and his demeanour suggested that we should get on with it now.

The opening pitches of many of these Upper Crag climbs could hardly be bettered. On high-angled slabs propped up against the overhanging mass of crag above, you can ladder carefully up to the eaves in comfort. Tiny flakes have pulled away from weaknesses in the rock and left a plethora of little pockets into which a toe or finger-end can slot. So, for 30ft (9m) I pulled up to an overhanging recess and peered across to another slabby wall. The moves looked strenuous and fingery. With a small wire under the roof, I leaned out on a Slip Not-type move and swung out across the wall on lay-backs into the groove.

The wind was rising, slapping wetly at my hands and face in a casual, malicious way. John called out something and then turned and hunched inscrutably inside his cagoule. His hooded nods could have been the result of shivers or of hoots of laughter. Was it praise he had called or scorn? Was he envying my position and technique or was he feeling it was time to quit? I couldn't be bothered to use the energy to call down into the wind and find out.

At the top of the open groove, I pulled off the slab out right across some rickety flakes to a hanging stance on the edge of an obvious prow. The position is superb, and much more preferable to the block and ledge belay away to the left in White Ghyll Chimney. From here, the crux moves of the traverse are in sight and a second can share vicariously in his leader's experience. I had left a runner just before the move across the flakes, so John's rope still ran up the slab.

As he climbed fast to reach me, I hung and swung in knots of tape on belay. In the wind I felt like an old prize-fighter on the ropes, hiding fatigue from his manager. John would know I was tired. The 70ft (21m) loops of slack whispered away wetly in the rain, well out from the slab base, and I couldn't take it in quickly enough to feed the loop and feel if he faltered at the points that I had found tricky. Over to the right, looking in, the Klingon team were still clinging to the crux of Gordian Knot. They didn't seem prepared to use the little finger ledge high and right to lean out on and then use it for the feet. I knew the feeling well: the move is wild but safe, and everyone must learn to do it in exactly the same way as everyone before because the rock gives nothing else away.

When John arrived, grinning and hungry for a suck on his steroid stick (he suffers from asthma), we shuffled close together on the stance and swapped some gear. He was obviously going very well and keen to get away. I described to him the next moves from memory, but he wasn't really listening, so I let him go. Two pressure balances between the slab and wall with right foot braced against a polished facet and left foot bridged on an edge and the world contracts. I held my breath involuntarily as he searched for and found the crucial hold – the four-finger edge for right hand in just the right position to enable the hanging ramp to be gained in a bold and committing move. In seconds he had found the next crucial side hold and swung away right, leaving me sweating and shaking in the wind.

When I came to follow, the ropes snaked slackly to my absent leader, landlord of the second stance. It is only 40ft (12m) to the comfort of the belay, but feels like twice that distance because space is shrieking loudly at your feet. Small people are at an advantage here. My 6ft 2in (1.8m) plus helmet were uncomfortable, crammed below the roof. With hands rammed deep as possible into the horizontal crack that seeps from underneath the roof I shared with everybody else who has made those moves, the fear of falling. The rock is polished by the generations of sweaty palms that have gripped and scrabbled. At moments such as these, the guide-book description, so carefully memorised,

just disappears. All that counts is what your body tells you is the truth about yourself and the rock – and even then, the mind will still construct its own big ledges to reach up for, blind around the corner, out of sight.

Harry Griffin in *Long Days in the Hills* recalls watching Jim Birkett lead the first ascent. According to Harry, Jim had made the initial delicate crux moves, but then hesitated and 'in a completely off-balance position . . . seemed about to fall'. Of course, he didn't fall and, as the collected watchers breathed a collective sigh of relief, Birkett shouted down: 'Did you see that? I reached up for a bloody hold, but there wasn't one there at all. Thought I was off. Never laughed so much for years.' You try laughing in this position – the traverse bobbles up and down. Now you're hunched and bunched into a painful crouch, your diaphragm contracted and your breathing stopped; next, there is a horrible, smooth, right-foot slide down a suspended slab that is grossly undercut. Less haste, less speed or you could be off, perhaps where Birkett nearly was, because this is where the Direct joins the original route. When you look at the holds you are using to stand on, you cannot contemplate a pull into this smooth niche from underneath. But the final swing around the impending rib is superb and the belay is just a stride away.

I arrived and started to relive the moves immediately, checking off my experience against John's. I told him of the husband of a colleague of mine who had been stripping paint off his roof with a blow-torch, but who had ended up burning the roof off. I wished I could have done the same to that oppressive bulk above the traverse. It seemed from what John said and showed me that he had found it easy and a real delight. He also seemed to suggest that because I had come into sight with open mouth and hair awry, I was hating every move and so he was very open with his re-creation of the difficult moments. But this didn't deceive me. I knew by the speed his rope had passed through my belay that he had found none of my difficulties. We tried to match our moods to moves by demonstrating the finger-postures and body-contortions we had used.

The Klingon team who had gathered at the shared stance tried out the same patterns in the air in preparation for their own attempt on the

Richard Brown starting pitch three, Haste Not

day's climbing. A team play follow-my-leader and then, when you think they will stand still to rest, begin to contort and make wild stretching gestures. They are checking that the stories of their moves are more or less the same, that they have done as well as each other. But is the rock or is the leader the teacher? And who are the taught?

The final pitch of 70ft (21m) moves left beneath a bulge and then straight up. Although rather artificial because it is easily avoided, it is not to be avoided. John disposed of it very quickly as I knew he would, but placed a rock too well in quite the awkwardest place. I had the excuse of a tight rope to yank it out. Above the bulge, the climb opens out onto a rib of flakes and a little tower. From the wind-whacked grass on top I could just see Lake Windermere beneath the tent of cloud, gun-grey, but lit by shafts of light from far over Morecambe Bay.

It was only when we got back to the sacks that I realised I couldn't get my harness knot undone and with my wet and fumbling fingers looked fair set to hold up the day's proceedings. Smiling, John reached out and helped me to unravel the knot and told me something I had not realised about myself. Apparently, when I'm slightly scared, I take a hanging stance to rationalise my fear and the exposure. The tighter the knot, therefore, the greater the fear. Perhaps it's the same with other climbers? As we packed the sacks and set off up the stony ghyll, I felt aggrieved that John had not only solved my harness, Gordian knot, but had deduced the knots of fear that had caused it.

At the loose top of the ghyll, just before we turned west onto Blea Rigg, I turned and thanked John for his help and for his lead. And he grinned and said that he had really been as gripped as when he had done the Yellow Edge because of the wind and rain. I looked back at the brooding cliff and at the traverse underneath the roof and thought of all the moves we had copied from Jim Birkett's first ascent. Then John walked on. I licked from my lips the remnants of a piece of chocolate he had given me and caught my tongue on the broken tooth again – the relic of a winter fall on Nevis when John had held the rope. Quietly I followed him into the Blea Rigg Maze behind the gauze of rain. Whose ever was the route we had climbed, our day had only just begun.

climb. And it struck me as we stood and postured in the rain how the knowledge of rock in all its forms is passed on by this child-like mimicry. Our need to make a narrative of our experience, just as children do, and pass it on encoded is, it seems, irrepressible. This little dance of mimicry can be seen on every stance after a pitch and in every climbers' bar after the

The Walk from White Ghyll to Pavey Ark

White Ghyll forks at the top. Leave the ghyll by the left-hand branch, looking up. The stream bed will be found to be a quicker and safer path than the steep rubbish on its right. At the top, in a little hollow, contour round in a westerly direction, making for the summit of the largest knoll on your left. A magnificent view of the walk ahead to Pavey and Stickle Tarn will be your reward – if the cloud permits.

The knolls are seamed with paths, but a line can be espied running north-west under the slopes of several large knolls directly to the most easterly of the feeder stream entries into Stickle Tarn. If the flooding and marsh is bad around this area, it is quite easy to go round to Pavey via the dam. But the obvious (good) path is only 76yd (70m) across the Bright Beck marsh.

Jack's Rake quickly becomes the dominant feature of the great mass of Pavey Ark ahead. The start of Rake End Wall will be found some 27yd (25m) up the Rake. It may be possible, but not necessary, to carry sacks on Rake End Wall, although the overhanging crack of pitch two may exact a toll.

OUT OF THE ARK

Rake End Wall (4b, 4c, 4b, 4b/c), Pavey Ark (H. A. Carsten and E. H. Philips, August 1945)

For behold, I will bring a flood of waters upon
the earth . .
But I will establish my covenant with you and
you shall come into the Ark.

(*The Bible*, Genesis, Chapter 6)

As we trekked in and out of the knolls on Blea Rigg, following a rough westerly bearing through the fine gauze rain-net, I mourned the loss of view down Easedale and across to Helvellyn. If there had been something of an Indian summer in the south, it looked very much as if it had ended here, just as we had arrived to work on the Ark.

Staggering down towards Stickle Tarn, slipping on the soggy peat and slick grass, we could see cagouled swarms of walkers slogging up the Mill Ghyll path. Clad in brand-new Gore-Tex suits or cut-down duvets and clutching Wainwrights and large map cases, they looked pityingly at us as we crept past them at the dam, tortoise-like with our homes high on our backs, round the rock-strewn path to the Ark. We thought they had come to stare at it, or maybe to scramble carefully up the loose and greasy rake that tracks across its hullside. Luckily, cloud and persistent drizzle seemed to deter the majority at the dam and, as we pitched our tiny

tent beside the noisy waters, we were alone when the heavens finally opened with a vengeance.

I had waited a long time to climb on this cliff, and waited on an act of faith as well as of friendship, because at most times of the year the big black gullies are damp and dripping and the cliff itself is green. But when the sun shines long enough, the 100ft (30m) ribs of grim, grey rock between the gullies stand out proud and fine. They always remind me of bulkier versions of those other grinning ribs on that other Ark (as old as stone now), lost somewhere on Ararat. This cliff looks just like a boat capsized above the tarn, heeled over for careening, or dry-docked for casual visitors to come and pry at as they wish. But on its boiler-plated walls and slabs lie some of the finest and least talked about climbs in Lakeland.

This is also a place where names are talismanic: they mean shapes as well as things. The peaks around the tarn have strange titles, provocative of thought. If you walk past the Pikes – their sharpened profiles resembling a stickleback's spines – you come in turn to Pavey Ark, Thunacar Knott, High Raise and Sergeant Man. What do they mean, these names, one wonders? What correspondences between language and the land are formed here and why? Well, 'Ark' for one is a lovely word, redolent of hope, security and solid trust. Derived, perhaps, from Old Norse for shieling, it probably has a deeper ancestry than that.

'Pavey' may mean 'Pavia', the lovely name of a girl who is framed within a thirteenth-century deed of ownership to this fell. Whenever I see the cliff (its big black bulk is visible from far outside the National Park), I think of boats and of that long-dead girl called Pavia as she trod the berried terraces in search of sheep.

The route we had come so far out in the rain to climb is Arnold Carsten's Rake End Wall. Although rather short at 180ft (55m), it demands a great deal of energy and technique. The Cram, Eilbeck and Roper guide describes it thus, and all non-climbers will recognise it by its position exactly at the start of Jack's Rake: 'This magnificent climb takes the steep pillar immediately right of Rake End Chimney. It is a sustained climb with varied technique, good protection and perfect rock.' Climbed in 1945, a month before Arthur Dolphin's similarly graded Nocturne on Gimmer Crag, it is a tougher proposition than that climb and also one of the very few hard routes of the year that wasn't put up by one of the regulars, Birkett, Dolphin and Peascod. With little in the way of natural protection, each pitch for Carsten must have been a true test of strength and nerve even if he was climbing the route in the sun.

John stepped out of muddy pools on the Rake at half-past three after we had dozed in the tent while the rain was heavy. The small and greasy holds he held immediately were cold and lichen-covered. He inched across the pillar-face towards a flake. I tried to feed him rope smoothly through the belay plate, but only managed to soak my breeches with squeezed puddle as the ropes were mangled through the 'friction device'. I watched him carefully as he oozed slowly to the first protection on the pitch, his new sticky boots hissing bubbles through their lace holes as they squirted the slime off the little holds. Higher up the ragged crack that followed, he swung sensationally round to the right to belay below a bulge on a thread beside a shield-sized flake. I climbed swiftly up to meet him, cold and wet, shouting my address to a kindly photographer who had braved the rain to watch us. The move across the base of the flake was wildly exciting: a finger edge at full stretch for the right hand and I could swing across to a ledge of just 4sq ft (0.4m^2) and fit all our four feet in. The ropes hung limp and dripping in the carcass of a sheep.

The next twenty minutes passed slowly as John went up and down the overhanging crack, the crux. It was packed with moss and mud. Some walkers on the Rake shouted up to ask us what we thought we were doing in the rain. I told a momentarily puzzled John to take no notice and to hurry up and solve the puzzle of the crack. They were unbelievers anyway, unconverted to the vertical and they soon grew tired of gently taunting us and pointing out our folly when squalls of sleet blew in across the tarn. It was only September, but it looked as if the floods were nigh. I kept quiet and shuffled on the stance, praying for a sign that we were doing this the right way. Then, as the squall blew out, John found the tiny left-hand hold that helps the high step up the impending wall and disappeared from sight. I, however, needed tension to overcome the wet 4c moves up the overhanging crack.

In torrential rain, I tried to follow pitch three. A wobbly step left off the end of the sloping ledge onto a lichen-streaked edge felt very insecure; and sure enough, with white and pulpy fingers feeling nothing but the imagined jugs, I spun off into space. How on earth had John stayed on here? He held my slide after 5ft (1.5m) and I staggered back onto the starting ledge feeling useless. I had to ram my fingers down my shirt front into my armpits to get them functioning: hotaches and the fear of falling again brought tears to my eyes.

At the terrace below the final rib, a raven wheeled away with a guttural salute in search of dry land to the south. I stood disconsolate and watched it fly while John sorted out the balances up the last short rib. Light thickened. The forms of long-watched peaks dissolved and melted into the murky cloud.

The steep and completely frictionless moves up the rib were as hard as anything below. It was a super lead in the conditions, and I knew I could not have made it. On a dry day this outside edge must be quite literally a sheer delight at good 4c; today I realised I should have asked to do some building practice with the lads back home on the scaffolding in the wind. I wouldn't have needed so much faith in John and the equipment now, just confidence in myself and in my strength.

Thunder growled a Cecil B. de Mille warning at us as we finished. Swirling cloud and lightning completed the biblical epic scene as we hurried down in a frightening wind. The Haskett Smith horror show, Little Gully, seemed to go on until

The author on the first pitch of Rake End Wall (Richard Brown)

The author and Richard Brown on the first pitch of Rake End Wall, Pavey Ark. The route moves right from there to below the overhanging crack, then follows the pillar edge above (Sally Noble)

the crack of doom. The storm finally broke over us as I stumbled around in shadowy boulders big as boats, feeling for a dropped sling. I got back to the Vango last, soaked and sinful, just as darkness came.

All night the wind battered us. We lay awake and quailing at its Old Testament-type wrath. The aged seams of the tent stretched in the blasts, letting in a fine spray that kept our sleeping-bags well damp. A rattling in the dirty pans at dawn woke us to find piles of glittering hail in every greasy curve. Over everything, water prevailed.

The choppy tarn was gobbling further up the bank and threatening to swamp the tent.

Turning at the junction of the paths before the scramble over Harrison Stickle to Gimmer, we saw the cliff loom huge and dripping out of cloud. It seemed to float upon the troubled waters while all the windows of the heavens opened upon it and no bird sang. But we walked on wet and rejoicing without a sign because we had made our covenant with stone and with each other, and brought each other safe, down from the mountain, out of the Ark.

The Walk from Pavey Ark to Gimmer Crag

If sacks have been carried on the climb, it is a simple matter to strike up to the left from the end of the last pitch until the summit plateau and cairn of Pavey is reached. The path to Harrison Stickle will then be only too obvious, going south-west around the rim of the combe. If sacks have been left, it will be necessary to return either via Little Gully or the broad path which descends in an easterly direction towards Bright Beck.

It is most interesting to return to the summit plateau by way of Jack's Rake – a detailed description of which is not necessary here. Consult your Wainwright if you feel you need a blow-by-blow account of the path. But walkers may prefer either the path which leaves the dam at its south-westerly edge and heads off up the back of the broad slope between Pavey and Harrison Stickle; a prominent gully left again can often provide a sporting approach to the summit of Harrison Stickle, especially if there is old snow lying in it. Or, for the committed scrambler, a fine route can be assembled from the broken spur that comes down from Harrison Stickle almost to the tarn.

The view from the summit is its own reward. Unfortunately, next to Stickle Tarn, this is the most popular of spots in the area; so take the path which crosses Dungeon Ghyll as if heading off for Loft Crag in a south-westerly direction. Where the path meets the main Dungeon Ghyll path near a col and Thorn Crag, turn north-west until an obvious little scree gully leads to the top of Loft Crag. This is the technical summit of Gimmer Crag, so descend carefully down little slabs and steep grass in a south-westerly direction until the obvious Junipall Gully appears on the right. A little further down, the platform and huge boulder belay at the top of F route will be found.

It will be easiest to leave sacks here and either to descend Junipall Gully or to abseil down F Route to Ash Tree Ledge, followed by another abseil to the foot of North West Arête using the final belay of that route as an abseil point.

SLOW LEARNERS ON GIMMER

North West Arête and F Route (4b, 4c), Gimmer Crag (J. Birkett and V. Veevers, September 1940 and May 1941)

. . . for we have discovered that names have by nature a truth, and that not every man knows how to give a thing a name.

(*Cratylus*, Plato)

Sooner or later every climber has to go to Gimmer. The cliff simply cannot be ignored. For a start, the black North East face dominates the skyline of upper Langdale. Like a ghost ship sometimes in, sometimes out, of cloud, this face has a power to tantalise, to hold the gaze. Some 1,000ft (305m) below, a sighting of it from the camp-site will distract you from cooking or washing up. No matter if you regularly lead E1, the adrenalin will start to flow and muscles twitch as you trace the V Diff line of Gimmer Chimney from where it rises in a hollow place;

and, ignoring the stove, the dirty dishes and invariably the imprecations, you will go off silently, captivated, in search of guide-book diagrams and descriptions.

Secondly, Gimmer is one of half a dozen British cliffs – Cloggy, Scafell, Pillar, Carn Dearg, Shelterstone, perhaps – whose magnificent architecture has provided several great rock climbers with *the* line to set a generation alight and test the next.

As we learn to climb, we remember intensely the names of cliffs and important climbs that have been milestones in our mountain education: what and where our first Severe was; the moment when we solved our first crux move while leading. But there are climbs and crags – such as Cenotaph Corner on Dinas Cromlech – that at some point in our climbing lives we will have to get strong and confident enough to try. The reason for this is that, by some mysterious process, they have become a yardstick at that grade and invariably, *the* route of the cliff. Sometimes, these climbs become classics: perhaps the nature of the rock forms, or the first and subsequent ascents, or the nature of the first ascensionist, assure them of this hallowed status. Whatever it is, in the truest sense of the word, their names become known, by all climbers. And so it is with Gimmer's famous climbs – The Crack, F Route and Kipling Groove. Even if you serve a rock apprenticeship in North Wales, the Peak, or on sweaty climbing walls, these routes will keep cropping up in pub and partner-talk. They are touchstones, routes to measure self as well as other climbs and climbers by. And eventually, we have to learn much more about them than their names.

As you scramble down the slopes below Gimmer's North East face, there is little hint of the almost brutal superstructure of the cliff. Only from The Band, across Mickleden, can its dense integrity be appreciated: the broad plane of the west face is a whale's forehead, bursting from the waves of fell. But from the frightening, wet and loose path that turns north by east under the face, it feels more like being under a Dreadnought's bow, ploughing at battle-speed through deep turf. The much-photographed pitch that takes the great arête between the facets on the western side is a Birkett/Veevers' route of 1949, North West Arête.

Jim Birkett was a slate splitter for many years

and in an interview with Tony Greenbank in *Mountain Life* (September 1975), testified to the importance for him of finger strength gained from his work:

Anyone who works with his hands gains a strong grip; that's more important than pulling power. It's how you can grasp a tiny hold and hang on that's important. Once I get fingers over something, the rest will usually follow.

And in a wonderful photograph of Charlie Wilson belaying him on Kern Knotts Crack, Birkett shows what a master of this technique he was as he is almost riving a tiny flake hold with his right-hand fingers, fit to split the slate. His feet in nailed boots are slotted onto minute wall holds. Although the type of footwear he used on the first ascents of North West and F Route is not recorded, he did confess to a predilection for quarryman's clogs because, apparently, they have 'fantastic grip' and 'won't budge an inch on a hold'. Gimmer, he claims, 'was especially good clog rock'.

This combination of precise foot and finger work can be experienced to the full as we follow the two long pitches of these VS routes, moving from exposed and delicate work at 4b to more dynamic, strenuous laybacking and jamming at 4c.

My hardback Constable guide shows a leader leaning back to clip a runner in the wide crack below the crux of North West Arête – and that's a wise move because the traverse right from the stance takes you over a rapidly increasing void as the cliff swells. Drop a line here, and you'll find that by the mark, you are 60ft (18m) above the path. But every hold is big and positive; the rock, rough and honest in what it offers you and, if your finger strength and footwork is as good as Birkett's was, you will be through the bulge and out and wavering in the wind on the arête in no time. Here, the holds are smaller and the cracks thinner; but flakes appear for the left hand, good runners and, finally, a steep lay-back – the prelude to F route. Stay on the arête all the way for maximum excitement and technical delight. The wind thrums in the ropes like rigging. With hands to dance and skylark on the holds, you are

Moving right from Asterisk to the obvious crack of North West Arête (Richard Brown)

Stepping to the edge of North West Arête (Sally Noble)   *At the start of the difficulties on F route* (Sally Noble)

climbing up a narrowing mast. At the top, belays are scarce. Look well back on Ash Tree Ledge where, alas, there are now no trees, but only a white, wind-scrubbed platform, wide enough to hornpipe on in clogs, and a sound chockstone in a crack.

During the decade from 1938 to 1949, three climbers dominated rock-climbing development in the Lakes: Jim Birkett, Arthur Dolphin and Bill Peascod. Their output of climbs graded VS and above during this period totalled sixty-four, with Birkett providing the lion's share. Between them, they brought rock climbing in the Lakes through the relatively lean war years and prepared the way for the post-war boom. Jim Birkett, always modest about his own inimitable contribution (but not unaware of its significance), acknowledges that he was climbing within a tradition: 'You climb on the shoulders of the men who went before ... I was on the verge of the common man entering the annals of the sport,' and has short shrift for people who imagine he was 'different' from any other climber of the day because he knew of techniques that others did not: 'Jamming? Of course we jammed ... You use damn well everything to stick to the rock ... You jam, you press, you nip, you bridge wherever circumstances permit. It depends on the rock.' This is as good a description of F Route as we are ever likely to find.

The route, like every other Birkett route, is a powerful and obvious line and stands actually and symbolically between the easier clutch of West Face climbs, A to E, and the harder line of Dolphin's Kipling Groove. It is not a route on which to learn how to layback or to jam. It is an exam. The corner crack is reached either direct from the tiny stance shared by Hyphen and Kipling Groove, or by a circuitous move round to the right of the boss. It is then straightforward climbing to the overhang at the base of the corner proper.

The wall on your right falls plumb-line to the crag foot 500ft (152m) below. If you have prepared for this degree of Gimmer's exposure slowly, over the years, by learning and repeating the West Face alphabet with a supportive friend, then this revision of insecurity will be of secondary importance. But if you have not, the next 50ft (15m) will be a primary experience – a real lesson in reading rock.

Make sure of runners when you can because the groove and wall steepen at 70ft (21m). Footholds are available, but at a premium. There are two rests, luckily below harder moves. From the last, keep going. The rock is free of lichen-fall from the nature-table top, but it is smooth.

Lay-back with your toes up by your eyes and you will be able to bridge and nip the final block. But if you're feeling caned, take care with the finishing move. David Craig, who knows the crag as well as his times table (and should have known better), confessed that he was once so relieved to have made it to here that he took his eyes off the text of rock on the final wide step across the groove and fell 30ft (9m) straight back down it. Even small teachers, like David, it seems, sometimes need to relearn the rule that in the Gimmer alphabet of rock, what comes after pride in F is all of Kipling Groove.

The Walk from Gimmer Crag to Raven Crag

From the summit of Gimmer it is best to retrace your steps to the summit of Loft Crag until it is possible to contour down and round to pick up a clear path which passes underneath a small spring and across a beck. The path then contours in an easterly direction until a steep descent down little scree gullies leads to the foot of Middle Fell Buttress, and a little further on, the foot of Raven Crag. This is the path referred to in the Constable guide's Gimmer section. After climbing Bilberry Buttress, and a pint in the pub, a stroll along the river to the New Dungeon Ghyll car park completes the day.

SOUR AND SWEET

Bilberry Buttress (4b, 4c, 4b), Raven Crag (C. F. Rolland and J. F. Renwick, June 1941)

Chewing the food of sweet and bitter fancy.

(*As You Like It*, Shakespeare)

For many years, the path to Raven Crag lay directly up the hillside behind the Old Dungeon Ghyll Hotel. Over those years, the cleated boot soles of tens of thousands of climbers pushed hundreds of tons of scree down the slope over a retaining stone wall and cut the soft turf of the lower fields into deep, dry gullies. Ten years ago, the erosion both below and on the crag became more than an unsightly problem: without a binding carpet of grass, the ground began to fall away from the crag foot; the path up its easterly edge to the descent terrace grew loose and serious and parts of the crag itself began to look worn. Even the polished trunk of the holly tree that dominated the central groove of the crag, providing a belay for two routes, disintegrated.

Today, a carefully constructed path leads well out of the newly planted area behind the hotel, then contours round to meet the path below the crag. And although work continues on the paths leading up to the descent gully, the larger problem of damage-limitation on the rock of the cliff still looms. The reasons are obvious: with the advantages of close proximity to a car park, camp-site and pub, quick-drying rock, several good middle-grade routes and lots of sunshine, it is quite unsurprising that Raven Crag, like its smaller neighbour, Lower Scout Crag, has become one of the most popular climbing venues in the Lake District for beginners. Many of the easier routes provide day-long enjoyment for large parties of novices, usually to the delight and edification of the novices, but generally to the detriment of Raven Crag. Indeed, few of Lakeland's cliffs, with possibly the exception of the aforementioned Lower Scout and Shepherd's – the Tremadog of Borrowdale – suffer from such heavy usage. Crucial holds are polished; the friable ramp line which provides the belays for half a dozen climbs gets more worn each year and there are now no more bilberries to be found on Bilberry Buttress. In years to come, we may

need to leave the crag alone for a year or two so that our great-grandchildren will still be able to recognise the climbs which they first saw in faded photographs of the 1980s and find, as our predecessors must have done, all the fruits and flowers of the mountain.

Coming down the scree chute above Middle Fell Farm from Gimmer late on a summer's day, you will see the crag in shade and, with a little luck, quiet. A few serious soloists may be out for an evening's enjoyment, but the large parties will by now be cooling in the Old Dungeon Ghyll Hotel. It is the best time of day to get to grips with the strenuous bottom pitches of Bilberry Buttress.

The Constable guide says that although the route is 'artificial' in line, it 'gives a sustained series of crack pitches unusual in Langdale'. Now I must confess never to have worked out quite what that means, because over the years I have done many strenuous crack pitches on Pavey, White Ghyll and Gimmer, and many that have been the same sort of sour struggle, half-jammed, half-lay-backed, standing on tiny polished footholds.

The first pitch looks easy. But once you have leaned across to the start of the wide crack, flicked a long sling round the chockstone and followed it by a step to stay in balance, you are suddenly committed and will have to finish on fists, fast. There is no further protection in the crack and you will find that you quickly run out of strength searching for somewhere else. The final haul up and round the polished flake goes on for ever.

Get your partner to lead the next short pitch – the bitter-sweet connection. After another step right from the security of a big ledge, a steep, friable little crack presents itself. Again, protection is awkward to find and to arrange. You must grasp the bitter crack, pull up, savour the taste of strain in fingers and calves, pull up once more and clutch the sweet flake above. The shattered ramp is only 20ft (6m) away.

The last two pitches can be run together to provide a magnificent dessert – just what you fancy to finish the day's climbing. A few steep moves up the dirty crack at the right-hand end of the wall lead to the massive block, perched in a niche, a rest, plenty of runners and a belay if you wish to follow the guide's instructions.

Across the valley, in the camp-site, stoves are

Nigel Birtwell ignoring the crack on the first pitch of Bilberry Buttress

Nigel Birtwell completing the sensational last pitch of Bilberry Buttress (Ian Smith)

Pulling over the crux, pitch two of Bilberry Buttress

(right) Ian Smith stretched out on the final pitch of Bilberry Buttress

being lit for supper. Tired walkers, sipping slowly from pints of creamy beer, are draped, wrung out like washing, over the stone walls of the hotel. Shadows of the fells begin to take their places round the patterned tablecloth of fields. It's been a long day.

Moving left across a steep wall is delicious; the whole route is laid out below you. Small friction footholds are served up regularly, just as you like it, together with crisp, black handholds, set almost decoratively like wafers, in a line under

the overhang above. From the recess, your second is out of sight; so fix a good runner on an extended tape and step up to the last polished foothold and exposed swing round a bulge.

At the top, if it's the season, you may be lucky and find a tiny sprig of bilberries. Chew slowly on them, and their quick, sharp, sour-sweetness will stay with you as you run, like all the others have done before you, down the years and the scree-path to the hotel and that first sweet pint of bitter in the bar.

2 P·A·T·T·E·R·D·A·L·E

The Walk from Patterdale to Eagle Crag

It is easy to forget that Patterdale is a major Lakeland climbing area. Tucked as it is over Kirkstone Pass, and more often thought of as a tourist's haven for viewing Ullswater or a base for walkers keen on walking up Helvellyn via Striding Edge, it contains some of the finest and hardest of the Lake District's climbs. South and east of Brother's Water, Thresthwaite Cove provides some modern desperates; and a series of deep valleys running south-west into the Helvellyn massif lead to high crags and great climbs. The furthest north of these valleys cuts deep into the ridge that runs from Ambleside almost as far as Keswick. Broad enough to carry a road across to meet the A591 just north of Grasmere, it is a blessing that it does not, because otherwise these beautiful eastern crags would be reduced, the long walks needed to reach them cut to after-dinner strolls.

The three climbs I have chosen for this long day lie on two of these crags; they are linked by a 5 mile (8km) walk that takes in some magnificently contrasting scenery from the cultivated valley of Grisedale to the wild upland fells of Fairfield and Hart Crag. It is best to start early in the morning to guarantee sunshine on both crags. Both are east-facing, but Eagle is often in the shadow of St Sunday Crag.

Eagle Crag, Grisedale, is best approached from Patterdale. Park the car in front of the school in the village and then walk up the steep metalled road beside Grisedale Beck into the valley. The crag will be reached in an hour after crossing the river just after a sheepfold and a steep but short ascent. Sobrenada starts just right of the point of arrival, below a clean slab. Leave your sacks at the base of the crag.

A SORE BAND

Sobrenada (4b, 4c), Eagle Crag, Grisedale (M. A. James, G. A. Leaver and K. A. Brookes, June 1957)

Refreshing, the wind against the waterfall . . . In old age mountains are more beautiful than ever. My resolve: that these bones be purified by rocks.

(*Zen Poetry*, Jakushitsu)

By the time I had dropped them at the end of the metalled road, returned to park the car outside the school in Patterdale and then run as fast as I could with rope and gear for a day's climbing back along the southern path of Grisedale Beck, Harry Griffin and David Craig, two of this country's finest writers on mountaineering and climbing, had already crossed the stream at the sheepfold. Despite a combined age of 133 they were walking at Naismith double-plus pace, uphill, deep in conversation, gesturing largely at

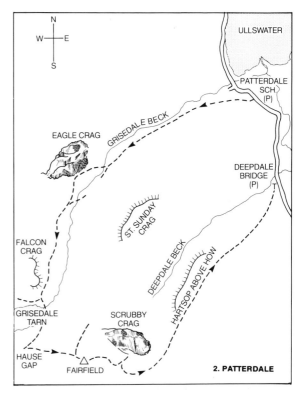

2. PATTERDALE

the landscape as they walked. But, having seen my frantic progress up the dale, they waited for me at the gate. As I panted towards them, I was rather embarrassed by my heavy breathing because they were leaning on the wall as relaxed as if they were sitting in armchairs.

Harry Griffin has been climbing for sixty years; David Craig started climbing in Scotland thirty-six years ago. Their knowledge of Lakeland hills and climbs is surpassed only by their ability to evoke and record these wild, steep places. I was delighted to be sharing in this knowledge, their memories and a climb with them because, as David has written in *Native Stones*, 'On the crag itself the old, the young, the middle-aged cross their purposes and even their ropes at times.'

As we walked steeply up the fellside to Eagle Crag, David's memory for guide-book historical detail, fed by hours of climbing, painstaking reading, cross-referencing and writing, was being checked against Harry's equally sharp memories of exploits with the Barrow Boys on Dow Crag in the late 1920s. Both men's recall and recounting of these events, from different perspectives, is almost total. It is also characterised, as is the

The author stepping off the pinnacle onto the upper wall of Sobrenada's second pitch (David Craig)

best of their writing, by a deep, though unobtrusive, romanticism and an almost schoolboyish sense of physical fun. I found myself in the middle of a recreative narrative. Harry was positively glowing with delight reliving the moments while David impishly asked all the right questions. Harry has a seemingly inexhaustible supply of anecdotes about these pre-war climbs and climbers which kept us laughing all the way to the crag.

Now the plan had been that David and I would climb Sobrenada while Harry took some photographs. And then, if we had time and Harry's feet were up to it, he would accompany David on an ascent of Kestrel Wall. 'All my best routes seemed to be called something wall,' Harry observed as he fiddled with my automatic camera. 'You know I pointed Jim Birkett at this little line – the last of his climbs named after birds? Indeed, the last of his new routes, I think.' David confirmed that this was so, then asked what it had been like, climbing with Birkett. 'He was very strong and

A young Harold Drasdo contemplates the move onto the pinnacle, pitch two, Sobrenada (Drasdo Collection)

(right) *Entering the crux groove, pitch two, Sobrenada* (Drasdo Collection)

very steady, one of the best and safest of climbers,' Harry replied immediately. 'Now, young Tim, how do I operate this thing?'

There is still something of the Lieutenant Colonel in Harry Griffin. It is unmistakably in his bearing and tone of voice, although there is nothing Blimpish about him – quite the opposite in fact. You know immediately that he respects and admires genuine response and achievement in others and you can see he also has the natural leader's intuitive ability to draw attention to others' strengths while playing down his own. But even though he revels in describing his own delight in naked bathing in Lakeland pools and streams and stresses in his writing the important freedoms to be found in the hills, he has strong ideas about the training and discipline needed for the demanding sport of mountaineering. Fitness is one thing I had already discovered he takes for granted; but he also feels strongly about people doing things correctly in the hills. Occasional passages of his writing, for instance, convey his bafflement and exasperation with ill-led or ill-equipped parties in inappropriate places. Taught painstakingly by experts to climb in the era when the maxim was: 'The leader never falls', I suspect he finds the current practice of climbers 'yo-yoing' – taking 'calculated' falls while leading – quite bizarre.

Thinking on these things under his calm, appraising gaze, I managed to make a mess of getting off the ground. 'Is Tim climbing?' David called down from the terrace belay to the strategically sited Harry, just at the most inopportune moment. 'Well, he's just fallen off!' Harry exclaimed, obviously as surprised (but nowhere near as annoyed) as I was.

Sobrenada lies on the clean, south crag of Eagle, to the right of Kestrel Wall. The first pitch takes a band of slabs, followed by a steep and alarming little pullup to, and out of a 'cave'. David had left one of his relics – old hexentrics on huge loops of ancient perlon – perched perfunctorily in the crack after the crux. Although he carries wires, he almost always never seems to place one until he has done the hardest moves, a practice which, when combined with his urgent, forceful but staccato climbing style, makes for some anxious moments for his seconds.

All the pictures of the crag make the climb look continuous, but in actuality, beyond the rib

of the first pitch, a large grass terrace cuts deeply back into the cliff, effectively separating the two tiers. I found David belaying on an old fence-post; it was his turn then to fiddle with the camera. From here, the crag is suddenly a different proposition. No wonder the Constable guide says that this climb is 'much better than it looks': I was standing under a steep and complex wall which ran to big overhangs and stepped, undercut corners, over to my right.

From some blocks I moved cautiously up to a pronounced overlap. A sort of pedestal spike blocked the way. It was puzzling. You could obviously go over it or under it, feet or hands. Was it two up and three across, or three across and two up? I was anxious to find the solution quickly, get established on the wall above and climb to Harry (who had set off on the scramble up the descent gully) in time for him to try Kestrel Wall. But a precarious balance up to the pedestal felt suddenly committing because it was steeper than it looked and the holds over the overlap, which would have held me well in tension close to the rock, were unfairly small. However, with a high left foot I made it, wobbling and breathing heavily again, to the foot of the smooth chimney and the crux proper.

This was the nervy bit. Harold Drasdo had told me that when he set out on an early repeat of the climb, he had been so frightened by the description of the smooth corner/chimney to come by his second, Mike James, culled from Mike's experience of leading the first ascent, that, after finding the overlap hard, he had lost his nerve in the corner and called for a top rope. He has regretted that lapse ever since.

I don't remember much about the corner; there are few rock clues given away, and even fewer runners. David said I climbed it faster than he thought I would, which I suppose is accurate since all I can recall is feeling appalled at how steep and smooth it was and how cold the water was in the crucial finger pocket, the only real hold for 10ft (3m). It looked from the slab after the corner as if the climb ought to continue up the hanging groove above. But the lay-back was clearly much harder than VS, so round left onto a further slab I went and the top was suddenly in sight.

Harry was sitting Punch-like, beaming at me. But it was obvious that if we were to get him home in time for his medical appointment, we would have to leave Eagle now. David and I could come out again later in the week to do the day properly.

It was typical of Harry that we hadn't been aware of how much pain his legs now gave him. I think his desire for the hills is so strong that it sometimes overrides the pains of ageing. In a recent magazine article, for instance, he blamed his recent loss of appetite and weight on a 'lack of strenuous exercise on the heights'. But, sore as he was today, he thanked us effusively for cutting short our plans and giving him a chance to walk and talk in the mountains. As we half-ran down the hill, painfully, to Patterdale, it came to me that the pleasure in the day had come less from solving the puzzle of the climb and more from being in the company of a man who, after a lifetime of climbing, can still write that '. . . the climber, after he has become too old and decrepit for the harder climbs, goes back to the hills to walk the heights'. May the desire for mountains be still as strong in all of us who love the hills when we are old.

The Walk from Eagle Crag to Scrubby Crag

Many adventurous walkers may want the additional challenge of reaching Scrubby Crag via Pinnacle Ridge on St Sunday Crag opposite. But for those who prefer to gain height, not to lose it, the steady ascent to Grisedale Tarn up one of Lakeland's most popular paths will not be unrewarding. A dip in the tarn can then be followed by a leisurely ascent of the broad but steep eastern slope of Fairfield and the traverse of the ridge to Link Hause. Scrubby Crag lies just under the eastern rim of a prominent spur running north from the Hause. If sacks are left at the foot of an obvious broken ramp coming down from the crag, about 100ft (30m) below the col, they can be retrieved after descending from the top of Grendel. The start of Beowulf is a further 100ft (30m) below this ramp.

The author high on the second pitch of Beowulf, Scrubby Crag (Brigitte Randle)

NO HEROES

Beowulf (4b, 4b), Scrubby Crag (N. J. Soper and P. E. Brown, September 1959)

The hero is the champion not of things become, but of things becoming.

(The Hero with a Thousand Faces,
Joseph Campbell)

To the north and east of the long ridge of fairway that leads from Rydal to the summit of Fairfield, deep coves have been gouged out of the mountain by long-gone glaciers. On the OS 1:25,000 map, contour lines almost merge where the concave back walls of the coves meet the ridge. Even strong walkers going champion on the Fairfield Horseshoe might well pause at this point in an otherwise uneventful round, look down into Link Cove and count themselves lucky that they have reached the turn of the ridge and these cove rims in good time, without the handicap of cloud. It is not difficult to imagine what a misread map, a misdirected compass shot or a mistake in pacing distance could do for the novice walker here. A dangerous drop into rocky Link Cove would leave you stone-bunkered, disorientated, possibly even hurt. And then, however experienced you were, you could probably forget about completing a Fairfield round: the only safe way out would be northwards, down Deepdale to the Patterdale road, miles off-course.

But for the ardent rock climber approaching from Grisedale, this cove in upper Deepdale contains a challenge it is impossible to ignore: Scrubby Crag. Tethered in the lee of Link Hause, with a sail of cloud billowing above it, it has the look of a weather-beaten longship riding uneasily at anchor in the buffeting wind, sleek, black and water-stained, but straining to break free from the hillside mooring.

The Constable guide gives several reasons why this cliff should be one of the most popular of Lakeland's eastern crags, and also several reasons why it is not:

This fine steep crag stands at the head of Link Cove and has a sunny south-easterly aspect. Unfortunately, it lies in the main drainage line of the fellside above and takes several days to dry

after rain. Despite this and the long approach, . . . it has some of the best routes in the Eastern Fells.

Jack Soper's wonderful route, Beowulf, is one of them. The overhang and curving crack of the route are distinctive, obvious features easily recognised to the right of Juniper Crack; but the approach to the climb is rather less so. Perhaps this is another reason for the comparative neglect of the crag – its verdant vegetation: Scrubby by name, scrubby by nature, presumably. And it is true that second impressions confirm this to be a high mountain crag with more than its fair share of mountain grasses. Despite the black plumes of lichen in the drain lines, however, and the occasional sods of turf on the slabs, the central walls and rough wings are struggling to shrug off the cloak of vegetation and celebrate steepness. And at an average height of 200ft (61m), it is quite obvious that had this crag been formed at sea level it would long ago have been a roadside attraction, gardened clean and covered in hard eliminates.

All the climbs are approached from a grassy terrace that in its turn caps 'a plinth of vegetated rocks'. Then, 100ft (30m) up, the cliff is crossed by another grass terrace; but as my partner observed, from directly below the central wall, neither Beowulf nor Grendel seem to be diminished by this terrace. Indeed, as we found out later, the terrace hardly intrudes on Beowulf because the flake belay at the end of the first pitch stands clear of vegetation and the route is wholly on rock.

On the day I persuaded Will Randle to walk over into the cove and try the classic VS lines with me, the cliff had been drying for three days. But, despite hours of easterlies, the great corners of Juniper Crack and Grendel still looked to be lichen-dark and oily. Quite clearly, if we chose to climb, we might just be in for an unsung, minor epic. However, before I could begin to think about what sort of climber I could, or might, become on today's routes, I needed 15 minutes to recover from the walk and learn the line. So, while Brigitte, Will's wife, carried our cameras and her six-month pregnancy easily up to a vantage spot, I slumped on a greasy stone and guzzled greedily from a box of blackcurrant juice.

Both Will and I thought that the conditions warranted an inspection of the route prior to a lead. It was a wise tactical decision, if a little unethical and unheroic. The first wall of 70ft (21m) is serious 4b, especially in wet conditions. Although it looks to be not much more than a climbing wall problem, a twelve-bore blast of black moss from the corner groove on its left has sprayed the wall with spore-shot, and every delicate balance move is a rock over onto these flattened black pellets which are embedded in the rock. Protection, too, is only adequate, especially on the little bulge that forms the (early) crux of the pitch. Until the good flakes of the groove are reached in 50ft (15m), you really have to concentrate hard on moving forward into the next steep wall space that your fear has told you will not be big enough to hold you. It is a lead requiring bags of confidence, almost courage, if you are more accustomed to the chatter and security of lots of teams on a valley crag than to the noise of winds and the brooding solitude of the high Lakeland crags.

From a small stance on piled flakes, we could look up the wet slab and overhanging crack that form the second pitch. This 100ft (30m) or so is still 4b, but like all good heroes with a reputation to keep, quickly becomes fiercer the longer and harder you look at it: it's best to get stuck into the fray without too much ceremony.

A cracked slab which hangs like useless armour below the shocking slash of overhang was very wet; so I climbed straight up a short wall to the base of the crack on good, positive flaky holds to where a deeply embedded nut on a purple tape beckoned. But when I got there, I was unsure about the sequence of moves and whether to jam or lay-back. Only a couple of hundred feet away, the big sails of cloud had finally blown out and shredded; grey tatters were flailing furiously over Link Hause. There was rain in the wind. I thought I might have to hurry.

Once embarked, lay-backing, I was committed. Every hold in the crack is superb – sharp flakes alternating with deep finger locks. But the footholds on the walls diminish as the crack curves further left and I found I had to keep

going up and out, looking for a rest. Leaning right to get maximum advantage from the handholds and balance, I began to lose perspective: my feet seemed to be a very long way away from me, not doing what I wanted them to do. The air got noticeably denser as I approached the crux. Even hyperventilating as I hung from bones, semi-bridged below the bulge, did not seem to recharge the muscles. Strength was seeping out of leaky joints at finger, wrist and elbow; so I quickly brought my feet up hurdle-high with my full body weight on extended arms and, in that most exciting of climbing moves, where the centre of gravity is furthest from the rock, pulled hard, pushed down on nubbins and sank my hands into big flake jugs on the right. All the rest of the rising traverse was in balance on more huge, if rather rickety, flakes.

Will in his turn fought up the crack with rather more control; then we both agreed it was one of the most satisfying pitches we had climbed at the grade.

Carefully picking my way up the terrace towards Grendel a little while later, I had no difficulty whatsoever in curbing an urge to dramatise the experience. After all, Will had seen me faltering. The only thing to do was go and try another climb and practise hard to become a better climber. There was no question of actually *being* a better climber just then, of course; but perhaps going climbing in marginal conditions is a necessary part of the long process of becoming one. In the meantime, I thought I would simply be content to play the anti-hero role and think of the thousand Lakeland faces I have still to climb.

The hero . . . must put aside his pride . . . and bow or submit to the absolutely intolerable . . . Dragons have now to be slain and surprising barriers passed – again, again and again. Meanwhile there will be a multitude of preliminary victories, unretainable ecstasies and momentary glimpses of the wonderful . . .

(Ibid)

NO MONSTERS

Grendel (4b, 4b), Scrubby Crag (H. Drasdo and G. Batty, June 1956)

You make the world by whispers, second by second . . . Whether you make it a grave or a garden of roses is not the point. Feel the wall; is it not hard? Write it down in careful runes.

(*Grendel*, John Gardner)

The desire to go beyond what you know, or think you know you can do, is a fundamental human activity, as common as breathing. Little children reach out to finger and bring the world within their humming, burgeoning consciousness; and though, as they age, they begin to realise that there are certain painful, unattractive boundaries to their physical worlds, the urge to experiment, to reach out and know the ineffable, never wholly atrophies in any one of us.

This desire to reach out for the seemingly unattainable forms the psychological basis of rock climbing and mountaineering. Every climber seeks to recapture the child's innocent view of the world in which, although the world has quickly reared up and is almost out of reach, it must be grasped, and known, and understood. And this explains why climbers need to have and hold some useless rock, and then go on trying to hold some more. Because no matter how difficult that rearing up, or how skilled and confident the climber, every rock face or mountain ice slope holds new terrors to be quelled as the rock or ice is climbed and known. And in the touching of the rock, in the passing over it, a fusing of mind with matter occurs at those particular moments when the climber is both mentally and physically stretched. Ask for details of a climb from someone who did it years ago or who found it hard, and you are almost guaranteed a description of the smallest of the holds, because after such knowledge, there is indeed no forgiveness. The memories, especially of the failures, stay with you all your life. And so you go on climbing – partly for the fun and friendships, of course, but also for the potent heady draughts of adrenalin which help you to come to terms with your fears.

The grade of the climb often doesn't matter, or indeed if it has been climbed already by yourself or others. This is because the climber's other world (of rock and ice) seems always to be in need of redefinition, as if each hold, each rock shape, type or form re-experienced, can somehow assuage the fever of a restless mind. It is not surprising that many climbers, especially in their youth, find the constraints of a regular lifestyle and job somewhat irksome: some spend their lives in pursuit of ever more intense experiences of rock, driven by a dark power to go on risking everything. And this sense of being driven is a common experience. It attends less upon the obvious delights of rocks and mountains than upon an intimation of the dark side of the mind, upon that first shattering experience when a climber learns about non-being – about a violent death on rocks. For Bill Peascod this came twice: the first after finding the body of a fallen climber under Pillar Rock, after which 'The first wonderful haze of confidence' was blown away; and the second down William Pit mine after an explosion had killed 104 miners.

I have friends, competent at the extreme grade, who still take great enjoyment when climbing big rounded Diffs which they did years ago or which they could climb blindfold. But even though the experience may not be the same, and now is more like fun, they still take great care when climbing or belaying. It is as if they are aware of the penalties for a lack of serious attention (the needless and untimely deaths of Tony Willmott and Jimmy Jewell while soloing on Severes, for example), or perhaps their imaginations, always heightened by the contact with the vertical, no matter what the grade, are set free to play on the forms of rock and on the dangers not only in the rocks but in themselves. We all know that the crags can change from day to day; but they can also change within our minds. We often make the difficulties as we try to make the climbs. Wordsworth, writing in 'The Prelude' about his boyhood impressions, knew how the forms of mountains formed his fears:

Huge and mighty forms, that do not live
Like living men, moved solely through the mind
By day, and were a trouble to my dreams.

and David Craig in *Native Stones* devotes a chapter to what he calls 'the fear barrier', which is:

a zone of nothing, where you cannot be. As you

move closer to it, it may enter into you – you become nothing, your strength is cancelled, weakness hollows out your arms, your feet can't be trusted, your brain ceases to screen clear images, your balance shakes out of true, your imagination can't conceive of a way beyond.

The acuity of these insights is disturbing. They testify to the physicality of this strange supplantation of consciousness, to the ways in which the forms of mountains and, for David Craig, the actual lines of climbs can sometimes invade the mind and become the shapes of fear itself.

We know of many examples in the Bible, world literature and in the diaries and writings of mountaineers of the power of mountains to uplift, inspire and charge the human spirit; but there are perhaps fewer accounts of the darker, obverse power of cliffs and mountains to paralyse and sap the mind. Set beside the finest representations of this experience in which the hero meets the 'beast from the mountain' and comes to know it as an aspect of himself, rational accounts of how fears of mountains can become realities as hard as stone read curiously thinly. It is as if the pressure of feeling is too much for realistic writing. Only poetry, myth, fable or an epic, perhaps, can give us that insight into ourselves that helps us face

> *Those obstinate questionings*
> *Of sense and outward things,*
> *Fallings from us, vanishings;*
> *Blank misgivings of a Creature*
> *Moving about in worlds not realised.*

('Ode, Intimations of Immortality', Wordsworth)

Meet Grendel on a fine day and you'll probably wonder what all the fuss is about. 100ft (30m) of 4b should present no problems; and on the sunny day that David Craig and I met up with the climb at last, I was continuously surprised by every hold I got on the groove.

The first moves are the hardest. You can spend a lot of time here manoeuvring for position and advantage. A huge flake, big as a buckler, provides the initiation: a step off from its rim onto the slab. The groove is on your left, but 5ft (1.5m) up and 6ft (1.8m) away. We were climbing on David's old red rope, and I had great difficulty sorting out long slings on runners that would hold opposing pulls before I had the courage to step gingerly across the sleeping moss

The author and Will Randle completing pitch one of Grendel, Scrubby Crag (Brigitte Randle)

Will Randle bridges across the groove of Grendel

(right) Reaching the difficult moves on pitch two of Grendel in poor conditions

and face the groove. The walls are steep and seamed with broken scars of rock. The crack in the back is festering. Get in too close and the stink of decay will be a shock. The secret is to keep the crack at arms' length and your feet wide apart, bridged like a fighter. Face right, otherwise the impending left wall will overbalance you into a fall.

Bridge and bridge again and just before the bulge, when it seems that all the strain has been on your left arm and shoulder for too long, break off and move out to the clean rib on the right and a rest. Steep but straightforward climbing, well protected, will take you to the terrace and a threaded chockstone belay.

But if the crack is slavering after rain, that bottom slab will be at the limit of the grade. Will and I took it on in these conditions and found both pitches fierce and challenging. Above the terrace and a little chimney, a chunk of rock has been torn out of a corner joint, leaving a cracked rib. The approach is mossy but positive. In the corner, look for holds out on the edge. A finish over flakes on a bulging wall will give you pause for thought if the wind is howling and the rain has started.

And there it is, perfectly named. No monster for the brave and able in the dry; but when the weather is on its side, there is no one else around and the mournful cries of stranded sheep begin to disturb, the wall will feel hard. The little whispers in your head will start 'this is no rose garden but a labyrinth'; your fingers will go numb and nerveless and begin to slip. Then, no amulet or charm will stop the slow insidious slide of rock into your arms and legs and you will have to remember everything you have ever learned about other VS climbs to help you face your fear. Just remember that there are no monsters in the rock – they're in the mind.

The Walk from Scrubby Crag to Patterdale

If the weather is bad, a descent from Scrubby Crag can be effected down Link Cove to an indistinct path on the southern slopes of Deepdale, under Erne Nest Crag. But the most enjoyable walk home will be via the ridge of Hartsop above How. The ridge is easily reached by a tussocky, broken contour traverse from below the crag to the col just east of Blake Brow, and from there the path is obvious all the way to the telephone box at Deepdale Bridge. The sun will be behind you; High Street a Roman ruler in the East. You will be able to look long and hard into the secret mirror of Angle Tarn where it hides straight ahead of you. A hitch into Patterdale to collect the car, or, better still, a second car left at the tiny parking place beside the phone, will ease your aching feet after a big day on the hill.

3 T·H·I·R·L·M·E·R·E

The Walk from Thirlspot to Raven Crag

In the early morning sunlight, Raven Crag, Thirlmere, will look almost climbable and Castle Rock a pleasant picnic spot. This easy morning of only 3 miles (5km) takes in two of Lakeland's finest roadside crags. After lunch in the pub, a brief drive down Borrowdale for three more routes will complete a magnificent day.

From the car park of the hotel at Thirlspot, walk down the road until you find yourself opposite the hamlet of Fisher Place. A track leads west to fields and tractor-scarred paths which can be followed easily up and into the western reaches of Great How Wood. Eventually, the path comes down to the dam road and a turn left will quickly lead to the junction of the dam road with the lake road. A footpath leads up through the trees to the foot of Raven Crag in 15 minutes. Head for a little bay directly below the cave area and leave the sacks here.

RED RAGS

Communist Convert (4b, 4b), Raven Crag, Thirlmere (A. R. Dolphin, D. Hopkin, M. Dwyer and J. Ramsden, May 1953)

let's go quit it,
let's go across the river and into the trees
let's leave the red rags behind,
let's go some other place

('Bullfight', Miroslav Holub)

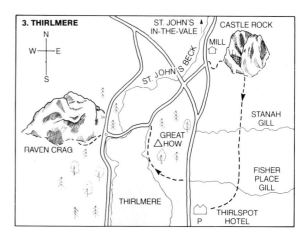

A pair of peregrines are mobbing a buzzard in clear air as we toil cautiously over the greasy stones to the base of Raven Crag, Thirlmere. Things aren't much better on the cliff. Days of Easter rain have produced a wide swathe of dampness, 100ft (30m) high and 20ft (6m) wide, sweeping right through the delicate crux area of Communist Convert from the thick turf at the top of the open groove of the Direct Finish. The big shield of grey rock which forms the open right face of the cliff is now a turncoat black. It is a good job that I have packed the big red drying-up cloth.

'Do you want to lead this bit?' I ask Terry when I reach the start, the first pitch of Necropolis, by a damp rowan. 'It's usually a solo scramble, but with the looseness and the rain, it's probably safer to put a rope on and climb it as a pitch.'

'No thanks; and anyway, you've got the gear,'

he replies coolly, uncoiling the ropes. What he means is that this is my idea and that he is happy to come along for the climb. But it is my lead . . . and my dish-cloth.

'I remember these first strenuous swings,' I mutter, as with feet sliding in the mud, I launch out up the tree-filled groove. Over moss and shattered rock I move rightwards to the foot of a green-glazed slab, putting in one runner to protect a wet step. At the stance, drips from the cave lip 40ft (12m) above fall lazily towards my upturned face, growing bigger by the second

The crux of Communist Convert on Raven Crag, Thirlmere. The author and Terry Gifford climbing (Sally Noble)

until they burst like bombs on the belay. I try to judge their destination by looking up their flightpaths and dodging into safe space inside these lines. But there are too many drips, and by the time Terry arrives, grinning nervously, I am soaked on head and shoulders from the thousand shrapnel splashes.

The cave leers down at us. Everything is green and black and wet and wildly overhanging. Discoloured tat hangs in outrageous places, tauntingly. A dizziness, a sort of vertigo that is both physical and mental, starts up in me as we lean back, trying to spot the lines of Medlar and Blitzkrieg. Dolphin and Whillans, both of whom made efforts at the right-hand end of the cave, must surely have felt the same about this place. Perhaps Dolphin found this route as an escape after an attempt at Delphinus? At any rate, as I set about the edges and flakes of the first slab pitch, the dizziness dissipates: going through the almost automatic rituals with the toes and fingers on the rock in front of my eyes calms me.

Someone has taken out the peg belay, so I tie in higher to the first peg runner and a Friend. There's no sign of the pinnacle belay mentioned in my 1959 Drasdo guide. When Terry is safe and comfortable, and has me clipped into the plate, out comes the red dishcloth for the little edges on the right. I scrub until they are as dry as my mouth. The first runner is another sling in the belay peg. 'Watch me, Terry,' I whisper fiercely as I seize flat holds and make a slow two-step right, up a little ramp into the broad-scooped amphitheatre of the face and the damp. Every edge on the route slopes up from left to right (or down from right to left, depending on your point of view), so Arthur Dolphin's punning name, rooted as it is here in rockforms, gives much more insight nowadays into the nature of the climb than do his other famous puns on Gimmer: Asterisk and Kipling Groove. To an ambitious but inexperienced leader of Dolphin's generation venturing onto those climbs without the benefit of modern nut protection, the experiences may well have been akin to stepping into a bullring without a cape, because Kipling Groove's long run out above the crux without a runner would indeed seem 'Ruddy'ard', and the crux of the easier route still tricky because the leader 'as ter risk a lot'. All of Dolphin's routes share this same characteristic quality, modern micro nuts notwithstanding: they wander boldly

The author stepping onto the start of the ramp traverse, pitch two of Communist Convert (John Baker)

(left) *Raven Crag, Thirlmere: Communist Convert crosses the crag via the obvious ramp below the cave to the top of the sunlit corner of Anarchist on the right*

out onto exposed rock and then find technically exacting lines out of the difficulty.

Another wipe, another delicate balance move and step-up brings me wide-eyed and warming to the mantelshelf and start of the crux. Boldness be my friend. I find some reasonable placements for RPs by dint of reaching and clearing mud. The loud clamour in my head, of a large crowd baying for blood, dims.

'I'm going to do it now,' I call back to Terry, not really convinced that I am. He watches my heavyhanded technique anxiously, ready, I hope, to take in armfuls of rope should I fall. The cloth flutters over the finger-holds again and again in a doomed effort to keep the seepage at bay. Here goes.

With fingers of my left hand in the water behind the flake I must stand on with my left foot; my right arm curved around above my head in imitation of a salute, ending in a dirty little finger-cling and my right foot up and braced on another little sloper, I swing slowly out and up and throw my left foot into the dirty water behind the little flake. I look back at Terry. 'That move's all right if you watch where you're putting your feet,' I call to him. He looks at me then back up the lake. I think he's fraught.

But the crux goes on; and this move is harder than the last. I have four goes. My cloth is filthy and getting torn. Does it work like a train-guard's red flag, waving danger to my friend? I cheat. I blow white chalk on the only right foothold and the tiny opposing left foothold. I tuck my cloth away and look down the length of my out-stretched right arm at the end of which is one flake lay-back hold. I think I want to quit now, but I don't think I can reverse the wet mantel-shelf move. Instead, I move upwards and right in strenuous and then damp-delicate moves, head down, blind, going for the possible stance where it's safe. When I stop on a leaning ledge and look up, the sky is still but the rock is wheeling. I close my eyes and feel elation coursing through me. I'm converted to the vertical again after a few weeks off the rocks.

The last moves across a cracked wall and over wet, out-of-balance ledges are time-consuming. I scrub the holds dry in front and then move quickly onto them. They fill up behind me. As fast as possible, I reach up into dank cracks and slimy holes, cam fingers, crank, lean into balance again and move up over footholds that slope into space. The last important hold is also the best nut slot to protect us both for the final moves. I sweat and mutter, trying to dry it with the dirty cloth at the same time as holding on and cramming a nut into its liquid depths. Everything about my attitude suggests bravado rather than skilled control. I get angry and shout silently at myself to pay attention.

As I make the last long step down into the awkward groove of Anarchist and follow it with a cold, wet, strenuous pull round a horn and boss of rock to the stance, I can see a red sling and carabiner dangling like a bandolier in the black matt of moss of the Direct Finish. We can't do that pitch in these conditions, can we?

Terry comes across slowly, needing a tight rope. He says that he finds it hard and that his back problem has cropped up again. We sit for a while and look across the river at Castle Rock and ruminate about the route, snatched out of season. We both feel a powerful sense of accomplishment; despite the damp and difficulty it's been exciting. Our words and movements have been clipped and cryptic, stripped of style, but we feel we have achieved something in the terse struggle with the wet rock. However, when we get back to the crag foot, young Tom and Ruth are cold and bored with sketching and bird-watching, and we are tired from the dangerous descent path which has avalanched in mini-Peruvian mud-slides. In front of the children we have no option but to strip off all our gaudy gear and drop the mock heroics in the mud. Real responsibilities and states of mind must now prevail.

The buzzard is still wheeling in extravagant circles above us, although the peregrines have gone. We pack away the damp climbing clothes and I sheepishly roll up the new Habitat dish-cloth that is now no more than a red rag. Then, we slip and slide some more down the greasy path to the forestry track and into the trees. I think that we all want to be some other place, now.

The author and Terry Gifford climbing pitch three of Communist Convert (Sally Noble)

Castle Rock of Triermain

The Walk from Raven Crag to Castle Rock of Triermain

The descent from Communist Convert is along an exposed path to the north until an obvious gully is entered. This is loose and unpleasant, but leads quickly back to below the crag. Retrace your steps to the dam road, walk along it to the main road, cross this and walk up a metalled track to the B5322. The stile which leads you to the path to Castle Rock is just on your right.

Follow an obvious track up towards the crag until a little path branches off steeply towards the trees. Cross the leat and go up through the trees to the large boulder below the crag. Zig Zag starts directly above.

GOING STRAIGHT

Zig Zag (4b, 4b), Castle Rock of Triermain (R. J. Birkett, C. R. Wilson and L. Muscroft, April 1939)

By indirections, find directions out.

(*Hamlet*, Shakespeare)

Coming slowly round the bend out of the woods around Thirlmere on the A591, you change down into fourth to get a good mile of downhill at speed before the abrupt right turn into the car park of the hotel at Thirlspot. Ahead, above and beyond the white hotel and a light-filled valley, the dark purple saddle of Blencathra rides the horizon, wedged firmly by a trick of perspective between the flanks of St John's in the Vale.

The pass through the split hill straight in front of you once provided an almost direct route for the king's messengers riding north to Penrith and Carlisle. The road they took passed underneath one of the finest cliffs in Lakeland which was, according to popular legend, a fairy castle. Did those hardy king's men wonder, as they galloped wearily into the jaws of the vale and looked up briefly from the muddy track to 'a tufted knoll, where dimly shone fragments of rock and rifted stone', if the rocks so eerily lit by a fugitive moon were truly haunts of fairy folk? Did they speculate if those pale ramps that rise out of the trees lead deep into the keep, beyond the thick portcullises of yew?

Castle Rock of Triermain, imagined site of Arthurian prowess and inspiration for Walter Scott's romantic poem 'The Bridal of Triermain', stands square hewn at the very entrance to the vale of St John; and perhaps, because in William Hutchinson's words, it stands 'upon the summit of a little mount', guarding entrance to the narrow valley and 'shews a front of various towers . . . with lofty turrets and ragged battlements . . . galleries . . . bending arches, buttresses' this 'shaken massive pile of rocks' has come to be called a castle because it looks like one. Certainly, from the main Keswick road, the northern ramparts would look to Victorian medievalists or horsemen riding by, impregnable without a scaling ladder, grappling iron and rope – the very place, in fact, to try the perfect patience of an armoured knight. But to the modern rock climber, that pair of obvious ramp lines rising above the moat of trees from right to left across the impending north crag offer exciting ways to scale the castle wall. North Crag Eliminate and Overhanging Bastion are two of the finest E1/HVS climbs in Britain, the latter being the route which firmly established Jim Birkett as one of the leading Lakeland climbers of his generation. But these powerful lines are something for the VS leader to aspire to after a few visits. The 1987 FRCC guide to Buttermere and Eastern Crags has at last acknowledged that Overhanging Bastion is a good HVS 5a.

But the view from afar is not an illusion: the North Crag is just as steep as it looks and all the climbs are VS or above. Many of the classic lines and harder eliminates take wet crack lines or faint lichen-stained grooves. The climbing on these routes is generally strenuous and technical, often bold and always exacting. So it comes as something of a relief to read in the guide the description of Zig Zag as 'an interesting, varied, well protected route, the best introduction to the North Crag.' The product of that phenomenal team of Birkett, Wilson and Muscroft, only three weeks after their breakthrough on Overhanging Bastion, the climb follows a slighter gangway left,

Pete Clarke pulling through the crux of Zig Zag on Castle Rock of Triermain

underneath the wild catwalk of OB, before wandering back right to find an entry to the huge slab which tops the North crag like the start of a tonsure. There *is* some easy climbing in places on Zig Zag, but there needs to be because the crux of the gangway is taxing and the only vertical climbing (in the top part of the Mayday Cracks) is steep, bulging and often wet. Like its similarly graded neighbour, The Barbican, the traverses are there to stop you going straight: start climbing directly up and the technical grade rises like the mortgage rate. But on the five separate occasions that I have climbed it, the straight bits have been almost as hard as the zig zag ones.

It is a green and humid world you step up out of at the foot of the climb. Even in winter, the vegetation seems to sprout and the old grey rock at the start of Agony drips verdure from a sphagnum leak under the Zig Zag gangway. Each one of these stepped faults in the bastille strength of the cliff leads deeply back into the hillside and thus the lichen cover is doubly assured by water drips and tree cover. But Castle Rock is fierce rock with lots of sharp-edged flake holds. Look up at the hanging pinnacle of Overhanging Bastion as someone is trying to make that tremulous step onto the hanging ramp and you will be struck by how many little replicas of that famous pinnacle adorn the face. They are there in profusion, as if the castle masterbuilder realised he must scatter them liberally to counteract the squat power of the upthrust northern wall.

The rising gangway of Zig Zag's first pitch you think will be easy: feet on the ramp, hands on sharp edges above – straightforward. But not until you have climbed the crux can you turn sideways to the cliff and use the gangway as it looks as if it is meant to be used – directly. Each initial move allows the right foot to be insinuated on the edge of the ramp while the left is forced at cramp angle into some oozing little pocket on the wall. Luckily, the crack at the back and the holds above the ramp are really good and you can tug as many nuts into a down and rightwards angle as you have strength to place. If, however, you have as much strength as Charlie Wilson had, and can bend two 6in (15cm) nails by hand until they break, not much of what I have to say about the limits of strength and technique on this pitch (or climb, come to that) will apply.

Before the crux, you can pull easily onto a ledge, arrange two Friends and contemplate the wall which has to be crossed to reach the continuation of the gangway. The gangway is also well out of reach because a chunk of it has fallen out – hence the wall and the necessary pause for thought. Now I have done these crux moves five different ways, five different times. On one ascent I found myself lying almost horizontal, feet on nothing much, right hand tearing at the crucial sharp-edged fin that appears to be the key to progress, left hand reaching up onto the gangway for what I knew must be good holds if the pitch was correctly graded at 4b. Sweaty and inelegant that one. Another time, with Richard Brown, and showing off in a brand new shirt and harness for the camera, I bridged across the wall, low down, to a tiny nick on the square-cutaway edge of the bounding block – the crux's lapel, so to speak – and then lurched up to the flake in the groove, designer stubble bristling with alarm. Not much better. The best solution seems to be a combination of the nick, the leaning flake, the sharp-edged fin and a semi-demi-lay-back-bridge into a left foot rockover on the gangway edge, followed by a full body twist outwards and foot-change. Is that clear enough? Well, they are the best directions I can give, even if they do sound rather like a description of the newest high-diving technique. However, it is probably best to ignore my roundabout moves anyway since my friends have never awarded me higher than 5.2 for grace or mastery. Go straight up for the sharp fin, lean out and go for it. Then, if you've done it right, everything except you will fall neatly into place.

But there have been times when, braced across that horrible little gap, I have felt it would just be easier to move out right along Agony onto a nice steep empty wall than to spend more long moments trying to sort out how to climb the Zig Zag crux. Doing it my way has never seemed quite the best way.

Pitch two is a welcome relief: walk down and along to the right to where a line of big flakes leads round to the tree belay on Overhanging Bastion, then cross the wall on the right by an awkward balance type of move to an easy angled slab. This leads to the straight bit – the 4a cracks. Ignore the splayed greasy crack; there are holds to right and left – big ones, flakes and spikes. But they are always wet and black and if you go too far one way or the other it will be desperate getting back. The crack finish doesn't help either (nor does the fact that all these moves are overhanging slightly).

Somewhere up in Newcastle there's a young lad who decided to accept my offer of a climb up Zig Zag one day while his mates did Agony and I was wandering around the crag foot full of flu, short of a partner and (still) short of photos. This was something like his second route, so imagine his distress when, after six of my attempts to get the sequence of these holds correct and going in the right direction, I asked him quietly if he would care to try his first VS lead. All the way up the climb I had been telling him which hold to use, which way to go, how often I had done the route, etc. I could hardly speak for shame at the top. Ever since then I have been absolutely straight with friends about the relative difficulty of those cracks.

The top pitch is a doddle – quite an anti-climax really. Instead of finishing directly up the evil gully behind the tree, a nice clean slab leads comfortably along way left, over the sterner North Crag walls. But beware! On a lovely afternoon of sun, Pete Clarke and Charlie Davis – good extreme climbers posing for my camera – climbed all the zig bits and the straight bits, but couldn't do the final zag. This was because the crag had been exposed to days of rain before our visit and the first moves up the slab were inches deep in fresh water seaweed of a particularly malodorous and unappealing genus. So, as Pete landed, quite unlike the fairy folk must do, bottom first on the rope stretch in a heap of stinking vegetation, we learned the soft way that an abseil from the tree to the mud is exactly 150ft (45m) straight down. The ropes almost refused to come when they were called, despite being pulled down through a brand new, very long sling.

In fact, it turned out to be one of those days when nothing works out as you hoped it would. Just as Pete and Charlie had coiled the ropes, the rain set in again. So, since it was 6 o'clock on a

Charlie Davis stepping gingerly up a greasy slab on pitch three of Zig Zag (Pete Clarke)

Sunday night, our next moves were predictably in a well-practised direction: straight to the pub for a pie and pint, then back home down the M6/M5 to Wiltshire and straight to bed.

The Walk from Castle Rock to Fisher's Place Gill

If sacks have been carried up Zig Zag, it is a simple matter to follow the descent path southwards, following the walls towards Fisher Place. Here, a large path will take you directly to the hotel for a lunch-time pint.

4 B·O·R·R·O·W·D·A·L·E

The Walk from Bowderstone to Black Crag

The lovely wooded eastern slopes of Borrowdale contain some of the best low-level crags in Britain The glacial activity here has left bluffs and boulders, little crags hidden in high hollows and big faces standing stark above the vegetation. This is a longish excursion of some 6¾ miles (11km) although the walk to Grange could be curtailed if necessary. If this round is combined with the Thirlmere climbs, a long and rewarding day will be experienced, and all of it in the sun.

Park in the Bowderstone car park below Quayfoot crag and strike northwards on an obvious path out of the trees to a little col. Fine views of Great End Crag can be had to the right. Cross the wall and head downhill towards Troutdale. Black Crag will be in profile above and to your right, showing the line of Troutdale Pinnacle to advantage. From the stream that bounds the southern edge of the crag, it is possible to strike uphill and at a slight angle almost due east across three becks to reach the lower edge of the crag's scree fan and a path of sorts to the gathering point below the cliff. A word of advice here. It is probably best to carry sacks on this climb, otherwise a long and time-consuming expedition will have to be made up the descent gully on the right of the crag or a descent and reascent instead.

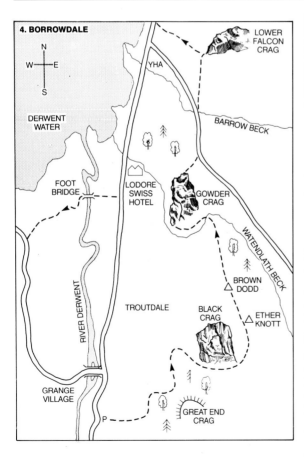

ON THE DARK STAIR

The Shroud (4b, 4b), Black Crag, Troutdale (P. Ross and P. Lockey, June 1958)

There's one kind favour I'll ask of you:
See that my grave is kept clean.

(American blues song)

Why is it that a fair number of Paul Ross's routes in Borrowdale have morbid names? If you look through the guide, there's hardly a major crag in the valley that hasn't been touched by this ghoulish rash. Names such as 'Obituary Grooves', 'The Shroud', 'The Coffin', 'Funeral Way', 'Rigor Mortis', 'Post Mortem' and 'The Gibbet' suggest that Ross, like the Jacobean playwright Webster, may have been 'much possessed by death/and saw the skull beneath the skin'. Well, it is certain that his potentially lethal childhood education in a Gateshead gang prepared him for the really lethal atmosphere of new routing and motorbiking in the Lakes a few years later, because we have his word for it in the Leeds University Climbing Club 1974 Journal interview reprinted in *Mirrors in the Cliffs*. We also

The overhang on pitch two of The Shroud, Black Crag (John Baker)

learn from this interview that Ross prayed a lot. He says that he prayed a great deal while climbing, 'because I thought if I fell off, I'd kill myself'. Praying was apparently 'a tremendous help. Every time you got to a crux, you didn't have just yourself to rely on. You just said a quick five Hail Marys and off you went, you never thought twice'. And he did fall a lot, sometimes hitting the ground. Apparently, he still does (or did in 1974): 'things go wrong now and again' and he nearly kills himself. Is this an explanation for both the death-inspired names and the presence of pegs in many of these routes? Given the hot-house atmosphere of the times and the fairly basic equipment available to an impecunious climber, perhaps he had no option if he wanted to put up hard new routes on the overgrown Borrowdale cliffs but to place bomb-proof protection – apart, that is, from saying a few quick Hail Marys. But if that is so, what are we supposed to make of this?: 'sometimes when I put these pitons in, I didn't realise they were extra at all, but subconsciously, it was Saturday'.

On Saturday, Ross and the lads went dancing. Nothing could be allowed to interfere with that. So, one Saturday, when he was 40ft (12m) up the Super Direct on Black Crag (a first ascent) and looking at an unprotected fall onto a marginal belay, 'the first thing that came to me' was not that he was going to kill himself and his partner, but that 'Even if I survived the fall, I wasn't going to be in any shape to dance.' I find that black humour comforting. It helps me rationalise my irrational fears about climbing Paul Ross's VS routes which still have peg runners in them and a reputation for difficulty and seriousness that is actually out of all proportion to their real difficulty.

Take a fine route like The Shroud, for instance, looking and sounding forbidding enough on the dark north buttress of Black Crag, behind its pall of trees and under a perpetual shroud of black lichen, but much more amenable and less intimidating than it appears to be. All that glowers is not bold; and of course, it is only VS. With modern equipment to supplement the ancient peg, the exposed traverse left on pitch

three is quite safe, and even the inevitable overhang (really only a bridgable bulge) and steep groove that follow are comfortably protectable. It helps to remember, though, as we find a perfect camming spot before the overhang, that in 1958 the only friends Ross would have had around him were either mild steel pegs or transcendental beings.

John and I didn't start the day well. It was warm and balmy, a delightful day to climb. Black Crag looked grey, not black, and The Shroud was dry. The trouble may have been that we were too early for a breakfast piece of chocolate fudge cake in the Grange café. It wasn't being baked until ten, so we walked disconsolately in silence over the col and into the quiet trees.

The opening 4b crack, though full of dried earth, was lay-backable easily because it was dried earth our finger ends were brodelling about in. The Percy Thrower approach to climbing (if you've got ten filthy finger-nails you're obviously getting to the root of the problem) clearly pays dividends in this natural drainage line – especially when it's well watered. But to the point. John wanted to do the Girdle Traverse first. I swallowed my annoyance, first because I suspected he secretly wanted to sneak off up Vertigo given half the chance and then I could cashier him, and second because David Craig had failed to get across the gully with Peter Greenwood a year or so before. Apparently, the gully was now in a highly dangerous state after rock and vegetation falls. Peter Greenwood told David that on the first ascent, he and Ross had simply climbed a little wall to a tree before moving right to the top of the Super Direct. On the second stance under the overhang, John scanned my old guide quickly and then, with the predictable impetuosity of youth, rushed off across the rickety flakes before I could tell him about the gully. Well, now I come to think about it, maybe I could have told him about it when we were roping up.

As I swung from the clutch of polished pegs, trying to find a large enough piece of my own shadow to put my quickly heating toes into, there was a fine view straight down the delightful bulge and side-step right that is the common second pitch with Shroud. Compact and relatively clean, it looked harder from above than it actually was. 'You're going to love this move,' John had said, taking his hands off the ropes to photograph me stepping carefully but excitedly

Black Crag, Troutdale. The Shroud takes a line to the left of the obvious horizontal ramp of the Girdle traverse up the dark wall on the left of the crag

over the black medallions of spores on solid incuts and nubbins. At the stance, I generously ignored the fact that there was 40ft (12m) of slack and that if I had lost my concentration on the very edge, I would have been food for crows in the trees below.

My reverie was interrupted by a scream of rage from around the corner: 'I'm going to bloody die here!' John had been out of my sight, but soon he was swinging back towards me, white with fear and anger, careless of the friable flakes, the poor wires and thus the huge potential for a sudden ground-embrace at speed. We didn't speak for several minutes. Then he told me that the gully was a death trap and querulously asked me if I had heard the noise of falling debris and his calls to watch his ropes, 40ft (12m) above his last runner on the traverse? I didn't say that I hadn't, but replied that I thought it would be nice to finish up the route we had originally come to climb and made some awful joke about the graveness of the situation hereabouts. A

John Baker pulling over the bulge on the third pitch of The Shroud

deathly silence ensued. John slouched off across the traverse and pulled over the black bulge and out of sight, leaving one runner as an indication of his estimation of the climb and me. I suppose he was thinking that Vertigo would have been safer and what a bore it was that I couldn't climb 5c. He ran out all the rope so that we couldn't speak and I would be unable to lead the mossy slabs.

Once over the bulge and lodged in the groove, I could take in the surroundings in comfort. The rock was strokable in places, coated in brown velvet. On the little rounded excrescences that were palmed to climb the second overhang, I was glad the spongy spores were not full of water and oozing brackish peat-waste. Apart from a leached-white scoopy ramp to my left that looked like an easy way off for both the Wreath and Coffin, there was moss everywhere. Every belay was a peg, and it needed to be in the compact, generally crackless rock. Climbing up this vertical rock-garden when it is growing in the wet must be dangerous. Ross had made his point: even climbing for fame and fun on unexplored cliffs, covered in vegetation must have had its drawbacks without peg protection. A peg and a prayer would have seen him up those ungardened walls, no doubt. And the only hint of fear that he might end up commemorated in an immaculate remembrance garden lies in the names he left us. If you read the Ross interview reprinted in *Mirrors in the Cliffs* and listen between the lines, you hear that underlying manic strain – the recollected pressures of being a Fifties roaring boy, a brash iconoclast who even from the comfort of exile in America and with the healing poultice of the years, could still score off old partners like Whillans and Greenwood. Paul Ross was the prototype of the modern rock athlete who is trying to break the mould and forge a new dynamic out of a received tradition, except that he used pegs, not bolts.

But we can find another sequential list of his route names that may help us to understand what it was like to be one of the best while wanting the laughs to last for ever: 'Illusion', 'Dedication', 'Entertainment', 'Obsession', 'Vertigo', 'Disillusion', 'Thanks', 'The Lastest', 'Joke'. What's in the name of a climb? Well, not much, except perhaps when read like this, as chapters in a book about oneself, a book about the fear of death and the rotten fruits of fame.

Climbing on the dark stair of The Shroud, it is possible to believe that great climbers, like great writers, leave a legacy for the next generation to interpret, learn from, and then leave behind. It is the way of all flesh: 'I don't want to be one of these old fogies talking about the past, but the past is the future because people keep bringing it up.'

Crossing the river above 'The Strid' on the walk to Gowder Crag (Sally Noble)

Ross is back in Keswick now, perhaps for good; the years of exile in America over. But let's continue to do him a kindly favour now and then as we climb his routes and keep them for the future, with his reputation, clean.

The Walk from Black Crag to Gowder Crag

The summit of Black Crag lies directly above the final belay tree of The Shroud. A little further over the back, a dry-stone wall is reached. Here, turn left (north-east) and follow the wall through marsh and bracken up a gully towards a col. Before it reaches the col, it turns to the left and you must follow it onto the summit of Ether Knott. This is a wilderness of heather and little knolls, planed smooth by long-gone glaciers. The best guide is still the wall. Follow it, keeping to the Borrowdale side until the distinctive little summit of Brown Dodd is seen. At some point before you are forced to make a dangerous traverse over steep ground, cross the wall and reach Brown Dodd. The views north to Keswick and Skiddaw are superb.

Go down directly north from Brown Dodd, aiming for a distinctive erratic boulder on a worn slab. From here, a little bracken-filled gully leads into a path system, field, copse and, soon, the sound of churning water. You are aiming for The Sluice, a strid-like narrowing of Watendlath beck above Lodore Falls. A well-worn path will then be followed eastwards via the stream to the ford and stepping-stones. Here you may be lucky and keep your feet dry. The base of Gowder Crag is 3 minutes away down the path on the opposite bank. It is best to climb Fool's Paradise with sacks on, ready for the next stage of the walk.

A SCENT OF PARADISE

Fool's Paradise (4b, 4c, 4b, 4b), Gowder Crag (P. W. Vaughan and J. D. J. Wildridge, April 1951)

Into a Limbo large and broad, since called
The Paradise of Fools, to few unknown.

(*Paradise Lost*, Book 4, Milton)

Everyone who knows the Lodore Swiss Hotel in Borrowdale will know Gowder Crag, at least by sight if not by touch. Clean and sheer above trees and the eastern bank of Watendlath Beck it stands, almost part of the hotel's garden. This crag and gorge, a felicitous combination of steeps and deeps, of water, rock and luscious vegetation, still traps the tourists into paying for a visit to the falls. It is, after all, close to the lazy lakeside haunts of the car park and the expensive comforts of the Lodore Hotel, and perhaps the modern sensibility continues to marvel at the model garden centre orderliness of the place.

Considering its modern popularity, it is not difficult to believe that this little chine with its cliff and waterfall should have generated so much interest two hundred and fifty years ago, and for very similar reasons: in the eighteenth century it was a model for both of those artificial interpretations of nature, the picturesque and the sublime. Armed with their Crosthwaite maps of Derwentwater and their Claude glasses, scores of artists, professional and amateur alike, would stop at this little bay, one of Derwentwater's best 'stations' for observing the picturesque.

Two hundred years of visitors and forty years of climbers have done much to change the aspect of the crag in the eyes of the ardent beholder; but what it hasn't lost, though, is its prelapsarian charm. Like its mythical counterpart, that other Eden, it too offers 'A happy rural seat of various view' and seems laid out on just the same celestial lines.

I first climbed Fool's Paradise – the finest route on the crag for me – some fifteen years ago with Ian Jackson. The route does not appear to have

---

Gowder Crag: Fool's Paradise crosses the slab at bottom right, then follows the obvious groove to the yew tree and the blocky chimney above

changed at all since then: the scramble right on pitch four/five is still muddy and brambly and the dubious block at the end of the crux pitch is still very much part of the crag. We had been attracted to the cliff all those years ago by John Hartley's atmospheric shot of a youthful Christian Bonington, tied into two solid white hawsers of Viking nylon with a monster steel karabiner, and swinging runnerless across a steep and flaky wall. It is the most evocative photograph of that delicate pitch I have seen and it still manages to inspire me.

I have always tended to start the climb at the buttress foot up a steepish little rib to an overhang, and from there by a delightfully delicate move using exiguous flakes for fingers to a foothold on the rib on the left and the first sense of openness above the trees. These are effectively the first two pitches of Gowder Buttress, Bentley Betham's initial route on the crag in 1947, and they profit by being run together in the modern idiom to give a warm up of 80ft (24m). The actual start to the climb is further right, but shorter and scrappy. The belay at the end of this first run out is a large ledge and well-polished tree. To the right, the crag is in profile and the bold slab looks enticing and awkward. But beware! Not every polish mark on the tree limbs speaks of belays: many abseils have been effected here because in certain conditions this paradise of rock is likely to prove a woe. Each crack and crevice, flake and incut can sometimes be full of swarming ants, moving on invisible highways up and down the cliff.

As I slotted fingers and toes up the rib then, I became aware that I was fast turning into a huge ant-carrier, overtaking up their road. With exclamations of revulsion and loathing, I kept pausing to sweep the red hordes from the holds ahead of me and watched fascinated for a while as 'down they fell/Driven headlong from the pitch of Heaven' into the deeps of green below the trees and John's hair. His shrieks and bellows increased as his own discovery of the little warriors was compounded by my gifts. I rushed up to the ledge, belayed and frantically brushed my clothes.

'I'm being eaten alive,' John screeched hyperbolically as he bounded up the rib on side pulls and notches. But once he was tied firmly to the tree, he calmed slightly and subjected every visible inch of his anatomy to a sweep search,

Terry Gifford making the crux move on pitch two of Fool's Paradise

looking for insect presence and assault. There was no doubt that there were fewer of the horny crawlers hereabouts, but we dared not sit down and plan the next pitches because we were mindful of the waiting armies by the path.

'This is hellish,' John muttered darkly, as he fastidiously slotted my ropes into the belay plate with his finger ends and fell to examining intently each yard of rope. He looked very unhappy as I edged carefully down and out across the wall. I don't think this was because he didn't think I could make those delicate 4c moves across to the dubious block with ease, but because his morbid fears of creepy-crawlies meant that he was stuck in limbo on that broad ledge while I was plainly in the vertical where there were fewer of the tormentors and (now) little purchase for ant or man alike. The pleasure of those moves across was visceral. It's worth doing the route just for this experience of balance and tension from slot to slot and from edge to edge.

John was still scowling across at me, still looking fearfully around as if he expected Satan himself in ant garb to land beside him. I was tempted to quote some more Milton at him, but wisely refrained and got on with the well-remembered crux moves. From a good slot, a delicate position on the edge of the overlap to the right is achieved by faith as much as friction. I found myself with both toes crammed on a tiny hold, reaching high and right for the polished finger edge that helps the heart-in-the-mouth move across to a small foot-edge. When smoothly executed without a pause or fumble, this move is for me the quintessence of the VS grade.

The author crossing the crux slab of Fool's Paradise Gowder Crag (Ian Smith)

Pulling out of the top of the groove, pitch three, Fool's Paradise

With a well-jammed wire in a crack above the block (to supplement the big chock between cliff and block in case this was the moment when they would part), I brought John to me quickly and then set about the open groove above.

The full stretch lean across the open base to a flake would be much harder should the flake decide to go one day; but the clean, well-protected bridging to a bulge that follows is as solid as cement. Steep and technical, it makes you think, and, like all good grooves, the further out you climb it, the better it feels. At the bulge, where a steep crack splits a block, the technicality gets strenuous. The committing pull round on to the steep and exposed rib on the right necessary to leave the haven of the groove is tricky, and then steep jamming through a bunch of flakes really dries the mouth.

John obviously enjoyed it because he kept quiet and said that he tried to think himself back to Chamonix where the flakes feel much the same. We were in the trees again and ready for the scramble through the vegetation on an awkward ramp-like ledge. There is a muddy move somewhere hereabouts where you have to change hands on a bramble bush for a delicate step over a hole in the ramp. At the end, I tied firmly onto a magnificent yew tree, sat cradled in a natural crook of branch and watched John as he worked methodically up the square cut groove and chimney. Beautiful whorls of lichen, red and green and yellow, were etched into striations of the rock in front of me. A patina of spores enhanced the natural beauty of the slate. The sun was a warm and dripping honey-pot. I dozed in the tree. Motes of mica dust shimmered, disturbed in the gently moving air currents and the slither of rope coils. Out over the lake, a light breeze was riffling quickly through a pack of ripples and wind surfers were pulling out their brightly coloured handkerchiefs of sails from the deep pocket of the lake.

As I bridged and edged vigorously up the final

John Baker braced inside the chimney which is the fourth pitch of Fool's Paradise

tricky chimney, I thought how well Pat Vaughan had named this climb in 1951. From the clear top, all the verdant chine below lies open to view and the trees seem to nod and bow their approval of the place in unison. We started to coil the ropes reluctantly, sad that the climb was over, and then stopped. Why were our mouths watering? What strange delights did this crag still have to offer? We looked carefully over the edge. An overpoweringly delicious smell of grilling steaks rose thickly, despite the dense green filter of the leaves. Down by the rare blue stamp of the hotel swimming-pool, a barbecue was in progress. John suddenly remembered how hungry he was and how long it would be before he would be able to satisfy that hunger on the heavenly home-made chocolate fudge cake in the Grange café. But with another route still to do, we could not afford to hang around indulging ourselves with fantasies of food just yet and so set off down the muddy path. 'Tis one thing to be tempted; another thing to fall', I quoted sententiously at my partner as we slid on a shute of slippery beech leaves. He ignored me, though, thinking perhaps not of *Paradise Lost* but of the cake still to come:

> Then wilt thou not be loth
> To leave this Paradise, but shalt possess
> A Paradise within thee, happier far.

The Walk from Gowder Crag to Lower Falcon Crag

From the summit of Gowder Crag, strike north and east, following incipient paths through bracken and whippy birch undergrowth to a wall and, eventually, the Watendlath road. Follow this as far as the tourist trap of Ashness Bridge, then take the obvious footpath along the contours to Lower Falcon Crag. Spinup is at the northern end, and a short scramble from the track leads to a tiny secluded bay below the rib where you can leave the sacks.

UNCERTAIN PROBABILITIES

Spinup (4b, 4c), Lower Falcon Crag (P. Ross and D. Sewell, May 1957)

Quantum physics asserts from the very beginning that no physical situation can be specified exactly even in principle . . . it is not possible to focus on all things at the same time. The quantum world is at root a statistical world: nothing is certain, but only more or less likely.

(*Physics, The Twentieth Century Mind*, Vol 2, G. H. A. Coles)

Climbing on Lower Falcon Crag seems improbable. Viewed from any point of the compass – south, through west to north – overhangs dominate the cliff. It all looks very demoralising for the middle-grade climber, and in my battered sky-blue Borrowdale guide of 1968, Paul Nunn sounds a cautionary note about the crag which helped me to forgo the challenge of an extended visit for many years:

The climbing is very serious for a small crag; at every point of the crag there is an overhang at some height. These bulges make one or more traverses necessary on most routes. In some cases the second man is poorly protected, and so a competent party is a pre-requisite.

Now, no doubt by current standards this warning is just the sort of teasing challenge a team might relish. But when you stand beneath the crag and look for lines, the breaches in that barrier of overhangs are not immediately obvious: some hanging ramps and tenuous gangways can be spied with effort, following what seem to be Skiddaw slate intrusions into the Borrowdale volcanic bedrock; but are they really climbable? Well, weaknesses there must be, and at a reasonable grade, too, because the Nunn and Woolcock guide lists eight climbs at VS. Of these, Paul Ross's Spinup seems the most obvious, if not the most appealing. It takes the bulging, steep clean rib on the left (north) end

---

Completing pitch one of Spinup on Lower Falcon Crag. Climbers: the author and Terry Gifford (Ian Smith)

of the crag, followed by a bold couple of moves into an impending, undercut black groove which cuts deeply through the overhanging barrier. Above the groove, a slab traverse right leads to a steep wall and the top. At 150ft (46m) it is a shortish climb, although it seems much longer for reasons that quickly become apparent.

As John and I came careering down the path from Gowder in hot pursuit of each other and the climb, we were suddenly clubbed into stillness by a hammerblow of sound. Two RAF fighters screamed past, no more than 200ft (61m) above us on their contour-hugging, computer-controlled pursuit of each other, the imagined enemy. Flying at that height, I remember thinking that there could be no margin for error, no second choice: the temptation of brinkmanship or exhibitionism a certain dead end. The echoes of their flight washed back from Falcon Crag in foul ripples of noise and filled our heads for minutes afterwards. Chastened by this shock somewhat, we started to change for the climb in quiet, but the question of who was going to lead that second pitch was still unasked and unanswered. I was more or less certain that I would be struggling in the damp and out-of-balance groove, so I gently suggested as we geared up in the grassy bay beneath the rib that I lead the balance and John lead the power. So in the end there wasn't any need to spin a coin for the lead. I set off round the rib on ample edges laden down as always with far too many expensive bits of modern technology, although I doubted whether they would make the outcome of the climb any more certain than if I had done without them.

Once round the rib, however, and from the left-hand end of a ledge, there was real VS territory where head control was needed for the compact, flawless rock. I managed a delicate lay-back onto an overhung ramp almost immediately and followed it, without thinking, by two brisk step-ups using flat holds. A polished peg winked at me from underneath a boss of rock. So far so good; what appeared to be the case from below was turning out to be the case. The evidence of my fingers, arms and toes suggested that I was well within my grade, enjoying myself and confident that whatever lay around the corner

could and would be coped with competently. I felt like a pilot steering blind around a bend, but sure and certain that it would be all right, running on auto, the logic of experience. John left my ropes dangling from the belay for a minute to crash loudly out onto the scree for a photograph.

A tiptoe right and up an easy angled slab and I was safe, tied into a peg and nut. John walked straight up with ease, then racked the tons of gear on his harness carefully, like bombs under wings, just as some walkers on the path underneath the crag paused to watch us.

Now I get very nervous watching other people watching me, especially when I'm climbing. It's difficult to ignore the impression that they're waiting for a fall. I got that feeling then, as John set off across the wall. From the certainty of flatness on an undangerous path they had stopped their walk and gathered in a gaggle of mutual support, settling down to watch us eagerly like spectators on a tight corner at a Grand Prix. Were they watching for a little lapse of concentration, the understandable human error that would send the car spinning or the body arcing into space? Or had they stopped to watch what they thought was simple human folly, gazing intently at us, willing us to speak about the vertical dimension and its secrets? Very probably they were simply admiring John's effortless technique and athleticism as he tried the combinations of little black edges on the impending rock above; and I was probably simply being perverse and uncharitable to them, annoyed that they could enjoy watching us doing apparently dangerous things from the security of the path without a similar investment of energy, drive or risk. All things are relative, of course: you can die on Lake District paths as easily as Lake District crags – if you slip in the wrong place at the wrong time. On the black page of rock above me with its whitened finger-edges, John was preparing to move. Let the rock speak, I remember thinking, and watched entranced as he made it talk.

After two finger pulls across the crux, John slung himself into the black damp groove at speed: it tried to tip him out. I leaned out on the belay and thus could just see round the jutty edge to the flat-topped flakes he was having to heave on to pull himself into balance. My mouth went dry with apprehension. It didn't help either

The first moves of Spinup (Ian Smith)

John Baker on the 'black page of rock' – the crux of Spinup

(right) John Baker on the traverse of Spinup

The path back to Grange in marginal condition

that the tourists had settled down and got a picnic out. The father could be seen distinctly, standing with a drumstick in his hand.

John was obviously in control across the traverse, 'putting runners on for me', as he put it, and making certain they would hold in the unlikely event of my falling after the crux. I shouted the guide to him across 60ft (18m) of space and suggested that he kept moving right until the traverse above the roof ended. But he had his own theory and chose his own evidence: no scratch marks, overhanging rock, no runners, so he returned some 15ft (4.5m). He stopped then and described the moves I would need to make up the black groove and across the wall to where he stood. I swung and listened, trying to take it all in, but was really too preoccupied with thoughts about those first moves on the black page of rock immediately above the stance to remember his advice.

The next 30ft (9m) were unprotected up a rippling slabby wall and inspired a whistle of respect from John, despite the fact that normally he would pass this sort of ground by without comment if it had interrupted the flow of a higher grade pitch. My hands were sweating when it was my turn to climb and I felt a pang of hunger: the tourists were onto fruit and yoghourt for their second course.

Everything felt very insecure spread-eagled across the wall and the bridge to a tiny edge on the other side of the groove was made only by an effort of will. I tried to repeat John's moves clinically, because reason told me there was little room for error if I was to stay on and retain some strength for the final wall. That it needed a quantum leap of the imagination to transfer from the out-of-balance groove onto the balanced traverse would be an exaggeration now, but then it seemed quite a realistic assessment – and there wasn't even any time or strength left by now for a rock-test of the crucial hold. Breathe; reach; grasp; pull; breathe again. I was above the overhangs, but at a cost.

Below the final wall I stood and rested and watched the tourists packing up their lunch. They bunched the rug up and flung it wide to scatter the crumbs. They had seen and eaten of the best and now it was time to move on along the path. I fingered the dusty ripples and tried to step cleanly and smoothly in a fluid style straight up the wall. By the time I got to John, though, undertrained fingers were locking up the tendons in the wrists and I had to finish fast. My legs and fingers felt as if we had done 300ft (91m) of climbing, and John said it was one of the best VS climbs he had ever done, which was pleasing.

Walking happily along the lake to Grange and our indoor picnic of chocolate fudge cake in the café, John told me about the plane crash that had happened here a few months before. I had missed it on the national news. Next day in Kendal, I looked up the back number of the *Westmorland Gazette* and found the front page details of a story that seemed improbable – a cruel fiction, surely? Apparently, two pensioners were walking on their favourite path below Falcon Crag when two RAF fighter planes had collided and crashed quite close to them. According to the report, 'all that remained of the jet that crashed – a matter of 200 yards from the pensioners – were small pieces of debris. They say it hit a stone wall with such force that chunks of jet gouged huge pieces of turf out of the ground.' One pilot was killed; the other baled out

and landed in the trees below Falcon. I tried to picture the climbers who had been on Lower Falcon Crag when the crash had happened: a second earlier or later and they might have been engulfed in the fireball that by all accounts had followed the collision.

It is impossible to predict the outcome of events with absolute certainty – we all know that; but no one surely could have predicted that on just such a day, at such a time, when two climbers were silently engrossed in the intricacies of a climb on Lower Falcon Crag, two jets would choose that particularity to collide in and sweep the climbers with their melting nylon ropes onto two tourist pensioners on the path below and into flaming silence. Statistically, the odds against a crash happening just there and then must be enormous – several millions to one. Of course, it is an uncertain world and more mid-air crashes may be just as possible, if not as probable as climbing falls, given the number of climbers and aircraft pursuits there are nowadays. But it would be reassuring to know for certain that as we climb or walk along a Lakeland path some things will remain the same – like Lower Falcon Crag and chicken bones, for instance – and that death will not come screaming out of the sky at us in the form of a Tornado.

The Walk from Lower Falcon Crag to Grange

The return to Grange is along the lake shore and main Keswick road. If the waters are high, it may be impossible to keep to the shoreline, and indeed, cross the field to Manesty via the path which leaves the road just after the Lodore Hotel. It is essential to be in Grange in time for a piece of chocolate fudge cake in the café; and then the car can be reached either by road or, more attractively, by walking to the campsite and crossing the river by stepping-stones just opposite the Bowderstone car park.

5 N·E·W·L·A·N·D·S

The Walk from Little Town to Miner's Crag

It is necessary to leave the car at Little Town for the walk up Newlands, but the scenery is so grand and the track so flat, it doesn't seem to matter. The track on the east side of the valley becomes a path after the Carlisle MC hut. After the spur of Castle Nook is turned, the whole of upper Newlands is before you. Miner's Crag is on the left at the head of the valley, perhaps still in shadow. It is reached in 20 minutes by climbing to the col and then retracing steps across a scree field. Leave track shoes and sacks under a boulder at the col or by the wall.

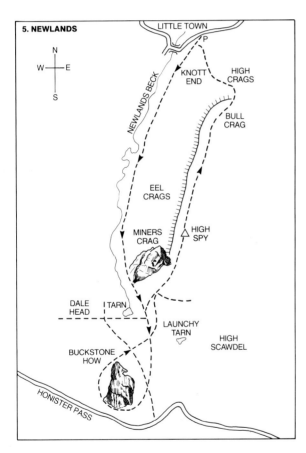

THE LEGACY

Miner's Girdle (4a, 4b, 4a, 4a, 4a, 4a, 4c), Miner's Crag (W. Peascod and S. E. Dirkin, July 1951)

What we call leadership consists mainly of knowing how to follow.

(*The Tao of Leadership*, John Heuder)

Discovering an unclimbed line on a crag is one thing, 'discovering' four huge unclimbed cliffs within an hour of a Lakeland road is quite another. But that's just what the climbing miners, Bill Peascod and George Rushworth, did in Newlands Valley. To the east of the path from Little Town to Dale Head, underneath High Spy, four distinct buttresses rise from a bed of scree. Until Peascod and his partners started to develop them in a burst of intense activity between 1948 and 1950 'These crags were all just Eel Crags. But we thought, we've found them, we've climbed them, why shouldn't we name them?'

Peascod's painterly eye picked out the colours in the rock of the first two cliffs from the north, Grey and Red; the next, the biggest, 'above the waterfall in Newlands Beck, was christened Waterfall Buttress' and the last and best, which offers 'three separate climbing areas', they named Miner's Crag. The name sits proudly on the new OS Leisure series, map No 4.

As Bill wrote in *Journey After Dawn*, Newlands is a surprisingly lonely valley for an otherwise busy area of Lakeland. It is possible to climb here at Easter or throughout the summer holidays

The last pitch of Miner's Girdle, Newlands, before the terrace (Brigitte Randle)

and, apart from a few parties of discerning walkers coming over High Spy bound for the look-out of Dale Head, meet no other climbing team. And yet the routes are there to climb: in the middle grades, as good as any on Shepherd's Crag, just over the hill, but without the queues.

Framing the view down the valley from Miner's Crag are the rounded Skiddaw slate slopes of Causey Pike and Outerside. In the foreground, stone spoil heaps – the lead and copper miners' molehills – lie forgotten beside grassed-over tracks, and the Tongue ghylls, unrestrained, leak threads of molten silver from the peat lodes under Dale Head. On a summer morning the crags cast long velvet shadows deep into the dale; but the light soon fills the grooves and slabs of Miner's southern face. And then, if you are taking on the thousand-foot (305m) girdle, you will be looking into the sun's eye for at least four pitches.

The 1987 FFRC guide-book to Buttermere and the Eastern Crags lists sixteen pitches for the Miner's Girdle, all in metres. The climb turns 280 degrees around the crag; and although it gets quite close at times to the rising ground below the cliff, we became so engrossed in following Peascod's clever line, that we hardly noticed that in places we were only a rope's length above the scree.

Will and I started up the firm southern arête of Newlands Gully in the cool, dank early morning. A fine, pale green lichen inlay on the rocks, rubbed off into my palms as I swung quickly up the first firm rocks. I think I must have left palm prints for Will to follow. The short slab with its tiny brick-like edges which took me to the first belay was a startling experience so early in the day. Will then stepped round the corner onto a gangway leading up across towards a nose.

'Is this a nose, do you think, Tim?' he called back after a while. I could just see a beak-like projection with a stone drip on the end. Will was sitting more or less astride it, much amused. Following his lead, I realised that he had run two pitches together. Neither of us was making much sense of the pitch lengths in metres (which vindicated my action of the night before when I had guiltily typed out the route description in feet). So, when I found myself below a little wall that led out right to an arête, I knew I was in the middle of pitch three.

Will was belayed beside a spike, smiling contentedly. It is ten years since we managed Centurion and King Rat together in Scotland – perhaps the most satisfying routes of our careers – but we were as easy together now as then. As we shared the leads across the face, we began to come to terms again with our different styles of climbing, thinking and speaking. All climbs should be like this: framed in the wider context of a long-term friendship and its rediscovered delights. The images we carry in our heads of friends who climb are like the images of our best climbs: bright and tough and challenging. Will nodded at the spike. 'Pitch 4. 8m. Abseil off a spike and pendulum into the holly on the right,' he intoned from memory. 'Your "lead", Tim, I think.'

Now I suspected that Will suspected that his wife was waiting patiently for this moment, camera poised, to catch her husband in a thorny bed. So I volunteered an old red sling (my 8.5mm ropes would never pull cleanly round the angle of the spike without huge damage and some danger from being unroped), the third I'd left on Lakeland climbs for this book, and swung off down the wall. Any route like the Dow Girdle or Great Central Route on Esk Buttress which contains a 'rope move' is worth doing just for that. At any other grade a mid-climb abseil would be either ridiculous or free climbed; but at VS, anything seems to go to keep the line intact, and they're always such fun anyway. On this one, I carefully pulled down across the overhanging wall to grasp a dead, white branch. Ducking my head as I reached the ledge, I was rewarded by the impotent scratch of holly spines on my helmet. Will, on his descent, however, didn't quite manage to balance the rope against the bush and suffered as a consequence. Since an abseil is hardly a lead, I took the next: a 4b wall to reach the belay above the overhang on Corona Wall. Suffice to say that here I really had to climb; and Brigitte knew it, too. I could hear the camera clicking on the wind 100ft (30m) away. The broad, quartz ledge above the overhang was as welcome as unexpected, although the belays were multiple to make up for their lack of individual strength.

Crossing the central area of Miner's Crag on the Girdle traverse

Once again Will took two in one: up onto a delicate slab and then down to sit astride another saddle of rock. I quietly thanked him for putting in the largest Friend at his highest point because the slab looked like an artist's discarded palette, full of oils. If I had done this climb with David Craig as I had intended, I might have found an old hexentric left to protect the move, but certainly not a Friend. David is rather a Luddite when it comes to modern nuts. I can see him now, shaking his head in bafflement and censure at my thoroughly comprehensive rack. 'You know that these pieces have moving parts, don't you, Tim,' he had said, the second time we climbed together. 'That makes them machines; and the crag has been degraded by mechanical things.' I thought that at the time he was merely teasing me, but now I know he meant it. In *Native Stones*, he writes that one of the impulses behind his climbing with Bill Peascod had been the urge to find out just what it had been like to 'push out into the steep unknown when ropes were short and weak and there was so little protection gear that a fall would be likely to injure or kill you'. A few times, they even tried the type of gear that Bill had used for many of his first ascents. His reasons are quite clear: 'The more we equip ourselves for climbing . . . with harnesses and nuts and slings, the less we experience the crag itself.' He sees the possibility that the experience of climbing can get 'watered down or impure' if one gets too dependent on masses of equipment. If you can climb comfortably within your grade, he argues, there is every reason to be circumspect with the equipment you deploy; and he quotes Jeff Lowe on the film *Cloudwalker* approvingly: 'The purest way, and the only real way, to be with the mountains is alone.'

Certainly, David is one of the most confident and competent of soloists I know, moving easily over awkward (mixed) ground of rock and vegetation with impunity in the same way I imagine Tom Patey did. Bill Peascod bequeathed to him the responsibility for writing up all VS climbs and below for the Buttermere guide. Working on it mid-week evenings without a partner meant soloing, 'climbing sixteen or seventeen hundred feet of rock in a few hours' happy work on Miner's Crag', for instance, getting ever closer to the real thing – 'nothing but the rock'. Although I never met him, I am sure

Bill Peascod would have approved.

The sun was well up in our eyes now, making the rightwards traverses a blind man's bluff with holds that were often illusions. I bashed across the dusty heather of pitch 8, sneezing violently, and taking too high a line. This gave Will the chance to combine pitches 9 and 10 in one. After he had moved under a nose and across another slab, he was into the clean steep ribs and grooves of the central area of the crag. I followed carefully across Corkscrew and round, delightfully, to 'a stance below a grooved wall'. Peascod's route-finding on these girdles (Eagle, Buckstone, Miner's) is superb and although he had the advantage of having worked out nearly all the vertical lines before he crossed them, following his line across these ribs and walls makes one realise how fine a leader he must have been.

I was stopped suddenly by the steepness of the groove above, trying to bridge as well. Muttering to myself about it being only 4a, I took the greenish, slabby right wall in three hefty heaves and moved around an impending corner out of sight of Will. What a view! A sweep of slabs abutted the main mass of the crag, leading up to the quartz terrace and the Jezebel finish. I tried to calculate how many metres or feet of rope I still had left before giving up and taking my turn at running two good pitches into one. Will did not seem to mind; and as we basked on the terrace and sucked avidly on packs of juice, it slowly dawned on me that he was going to get the final leads up Jezebel.

This climb is one of four of Peascod's climbs named after fallen women. Done with Stan Dirkin on the same day as the Miner's Girdle, he notes in his autobiography that it formed the last three pitches of that climb. Three pitches maybe in the days of weak ropes and few slings; but I knew 42m was less than 150ft and that Will would take it in one run-out and so arrange his runners as to have ease of access to the exposed traverse which is the best part of Jezebel. And so he did.

We were slightly apprehensive about this 4c finish. It looked a little like a White Ghyll move from the relative security of a crack to an out-of-balance wall and awesome rib. Imagine, therefore, our surprise, when the key to the traverse

Jezebel: Miner's Girdle finish. Will Randle leading the crux (Brigitte Randle)

left was found to be an easy step on a solid hold. The position round the rib was stunning – akin to pulling round onto the face below the crux of Kipling Groove. But it wasn't very hard at all. 'VS position, certainly, but severe moves,' was Will's verdict. And I had to agree. Perhaps the stiff finger pull up after rounding the rib was harder again, but then . . . the discussion carried on all the way to Honister and Buckstone Howe.

Bill Peascod's contribution to the cliffs of Buttermere, and to the development of Lakeland itself, was immense. When David Craig took John Baker and me up a new VS climb on Waterfall Buttress, I was impressed, looking around, by how much rock old Bill had found and climbed. David called that new route The Legacy, to record the debt he owed to Bill. Reading through *Journey After Dawn* recently, I came across the entry which records Bill's second and third ascents of the Miner's Girdle with David in 1982 and Chris Bonington a little later. He remained rather puzzled 'why no one else seems to have been there! One never hears it mentioned in climbing talk.' I wished I could have rung him up then and told him that we had followed his lead and felt we owed him a debt for his vision and that he should not worry: we would go on talking about the route, the cliff and the man himself to anyone who would care to listen, for many years to come.

The Walk from Miner's Crag to Buckstone Howe

From the col at Dale Head, strike south-west on a good path up the long dip in the contours to a plateau and posts. Turn west towards Buttermere and reach the fence line which marches up the hill to Dale Head. Cross the fence carefully and head down through spoil-heaps to some deserted buildings. Leave the sacks here and continue the descent via the disused quarry ramp. At the bottom, drop down to the right over a scree fan and the path under Buckstone Howe will be immediately obvious. Sinister Grooves is at the far end of the crag. A convenient boulder marks the spot.

An unknown climber on the last moves of the Jezebel finish to the Miner's Girdle

The penultimate pitch of the Miner's Girdle

AFTER THE QUARRYMAN

Sinister Grooves (4b, 4c, 4b), Buckstone Howe (W. Peascod and S. B. Beck, March 1946)

The hills went on gently
Shaking their sieve.

('When Men Got to the Summit', Ted Hughes)

As you walk over the dip slope of Dale Head towards Honister Pass, the tortured mass of Fleetwith Pike rises like a spectre. Its contour lines and shattered northern face are seamed with ancient trackways and gaping holes. Huge spoil-heaps dribble helplessly down its cheeks, almost to the road in places. But the trackways are silent; the quarries empty; the quarrymen long gone.

Buckstone Howe is another ghost crag. Facing Fleetwith Pike, tucked under the hillside no more than 15 minutes from the youth hostel car park, its stark ribbed profile pushing out of a sterile avalanche of broken slate looks famished, skeletal, barren. Here there is no soft turf cover, no lush vegetation; the rock is all you get. Bill Peascod discovered it and gives the best description of its nature in *Journey After Dawn*: 'There is a tendency for the rock to flute into vertical curving ribs and grooves. Because of its slaty cleavage, sharp-cut holds alternating with blank facets occur frequently.' At the base of the deserted trackway, just before you cross the scree to reach the crag, there is a walled-up hole. A prop is jammed into the angle of the fault just inside the opening. Whenever I bring someone new to climb here, we go and explore that horizontal shaft as far as we can, just to get the feel of the massive joints of slate and the experience of being under all that rock. E. L. Linton records in *The Lake County* that, on average, each quarryman made seven or eight journeys a day up, in and down, carrying 'about a quarter of a ton of slate each time'. The record seems to have been set by one Joseph Clark, 'who brought down forty-two and a half loads, or ten thousand eight hundred and eighty pounds of slate, in seventeen journeys; travelling seventeen miles . . .' The quarrymen lived and worked here six days a week, going home to their families only from Saturday night to Monday morning.

Peering into the roofless stone shacks, swinging casually down the ruined trackway and picking up this and that can sometimes feel like gross impertinence, especially in the late afternoon when the long shadows of the workings prop them up to face the sun and the curious gaze of motorists who are purring up the pass. There is a paradox here. The desecration of the hillside is severe: merely crossing the scree fan almost at its apex over thousands of tons of man-hewn slate makes one want to cry out at what we've made of the mountain. But this quarrying has been done because we needed roofs on houses. Men broke themselves on this obscure hillside so that their children could be fed. What tips the balance in the scales of history? The question is unanswerable, of course. There is nothing now to do about the disposition of these rusting cables, tons of waste and broken, empty shacks. And what we do now on Buckstone Howe seems almost irrelevant to the context of the cliff. The puny, patient wedging and pulling at the slate we do as climbers will be the closest we will ever get to quarrying; but it seems that when we climb here, we should try to remember where we are and who has gone before and why, just as in Wales, a route in the Rainbow quarries could be balanced by a visit to the slate museum to find out how men worked who had to handle rock to live.

Bill Peascod led Sinister Grooves without inspection, from the ground. But with his miner's eye, he must have known that the deep open V-groove some 100ft (30m) up would be the crux. It is 'conspicuous', as the Constable guide describes. Indeed, it must have been the challenge for the route. He reached it by a pair of parallel cracks that are themselves not without interest, especially at the top, where they combine at a bulging flake. The footholds stop and you must udge up as quickly as you can to grasp the big jugs on the ledge. It is all beautiful climbing, though, and if the late afternoon sun is on your back, the rock will be as warm as toast.

The hanging chimney looks frightening, a transplant from that wildly overhanging, slaty cliff in Wales, Carreg Hylldrem. It is obvious that

Will Randle at grips with pitch one of Sinister Grooves, Buckstone Howe (Brigitte Randle)

you must face left because the chimney tilts that way. Getting into the chimney presents no problems, but staying there does. There is one good foothold and one good handhold, but they are not in the same place. The left foothold is the sort of toe scrape you might use in an emergency. It looks rather like that hold on the slab of Birkett's brilliant Slab and Groove on Scafell. In Ian Roper's evocative photograph of that climb, the second is fastidiously exploring the frictional properties of this hole, obviously in a state of total disbelief. The Sinister foothold is just like that, a most unusual formation in an otherwise smooth groove. Perhaps some quarryman had a joke and tapped it out to lure the unsuspecting into the vertical lode. When John Baker and I shinned up the chimney, neither of us could believe the tenuousness of the move: left foot at full stretch and the right foot braced up buttock-high behind to hold the tension just so. Bill Peascod recommended swivelling to reach the top where a jug hold lurks on the right wall. But to get there you have to do some friction palming and some positive climbing in the corner to build up the impetus to turn around.

Look carefully at the crag picture in the Constable guide before you start the next pitch. John pulled out right at the top of the groove and committed us to some desperate climbing up thin cracks in a corner. The stance leads to a hanging vegetable patch of squeaky plants on the left; but you must step up right onto the rib and move carefully to a fine stance below another groove. This one is a quarryman's pitch, a perfect seam line running deep into the hill. And once again, it is harder than it looks: smooth, strenuous and slightly bulging. For 100ft (30m) you must pull on fins and fans of rock that are set like records in a rack. I was thankful that the ropes ran smoothly up the chimney bed because a kink catching across one of these blades under pressure would bacon slice the nylon in a trice. Suddenly, the route finishes in some slates, and you feel as if you're stuck out on a roof which needs a builder very quickly.

Walking back to the old cart ramp, across the eaves of deep blue slate, our clumsy stumbles on the piles of slate set them off in a stone song, rapping and clonking like old iron. We tried to pick up and carry the biggest armful of slate we could glean from the castings. But, like a clumsy novice on a children's game show, we could not hold the unaccustomed weight and shapes. The spilling slates smashed and crackled into small shards which were sieved into the heap and we hurried on. I wanted to stop before we set off back to Newlands, shout into the shacks, rock the rusty wires, anything to make the place feel less than what it looks like: a vast, forgotten, outdoor museum. Turning at the fence, I could see a silver sliver of Buttermere like a satellite dish, turning the message of the lake into airwaves and Birkness Coombe folded in upon itself in shadow. In this new age after the quarryman, only the grass splits slate, in Ted Hughes' words, only the sheep hear 'the stones cry out under the horizons'.

The Walk from Buckstone Howe to Little Town

From the top of the climb, first find the ruined cottage where you left the sacks and then retrace your steps to Dale Head col. If you are tired or the weather is foul, it is a simple matter to return down Newlands vale to Little Town; but it is much more satisfying to make a little effort to reach the summit of High Spy and follow the ridge northwards all the way to Maiden Moor. The views of Skiddaw and all of Borrowdale are worth the effort at the day's end.

Avoid Bull Crag by a slight north-easterly detour until it is obvious that easy slopes lead finally to the broken ground above Little Town. Pick a route through these little outcrops to the gate and car.

Buckstone Howe: Sinister Grooves takes the obvious line on the left edge of the crag

(overleaf) *John Baker bridging from the only foothold on the crux of Sinister Grooves*

6 B·U·T·T·E·R·M·E·R·E

The Walk from Gatesgarth to Grey Crag

Birkness Coombe dominates Buttermere. From Gatesgarth it looks big enough to hold a town. The path to Grey Crag follows the track across fields above the lake and then turns right up the fellside. Continue under two small crags to boggy ground and a little later a stile which leads into the upper coombe. For Grey Crag it is possible to continue steeply up the hillside on the right, through heather and broken ground before dropping back to the left and the foot of Harrow Buttress, the lowest of the Grey Crags. This approach avoids the tiresome scree.

It is best to carry sacks with you on the first three routes, thus saving irritating, though short descents. From the top of Harrow Buttress, an earthy gully runs down to the right to join the wide ramp leading to the foot of Fortiter. From the top of Fortiter, the foot of Dexter Wall is obvious.

THREADS

Spider Wall (4b, 4b), Grey Crag (W. Peascod and G. G. Mcphee, August 1945)

It bides there, quintessence of direction,
Absolute only path from here to there.

('Lifeline', David Craig)

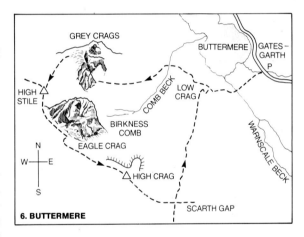

Grey Crag in Birkness Coombe offers the middle-grade climber some of the finest high mountain rock climbing in the Lakes. Four distinct buttresses stand out from scree and broken fellside under the summit rim of High Stile. In the early morning they look like natural solar panels aimed by the mountain at the sun.

For many years, the only routes lay up the ridges and arêtes. The Oxford and Cambridge Direct climb on the buttress of that name provides one of the most satisfying and testing of first Severe leads, on perfect rock. But from 1941, Bill Peascod and Bert Beck explored the walls that fall from these ridges and arêtes. W. Heaton-Cooper's beautiful line drawing of the buttresses, shaded slate grey by a fine slate pencil, in the Rushworth/Peascod FRCC guidebook to Buttermere of 1949, shows in detail how this team of scholar and miner, together with their friends, approached the job: Harrow Wall, Spider Wall, Long Tom, Suaviter, Fortiter, Slabs West, Grey Chain and Dexter Wall. Nearly every face route of note fell to Peascod's drive.

Spider Wall starts just to the right of the toe of Harrow Buttress, the lowest of the four. Bill records that he was intrigued by the obvious leaning crack which goes up behind the huge, almost detached pinnacle on the front of Harrow Buttress. The standard Diff takes the left-hand groove; Peascod reasoned that a strenuous start up the right-hand crack could be linked to a more delicate second pitch that would then wander boldly across the upper slab. In August 1945, Bill, together with the dynamic 'discoverer' of Castle Rock of Triermain and first ascensionist of Deer Bield Crack, Dr Graham Mcphee, had a long day in the sun and climbed Spider Wall, Rib and Wall and Long Tom. Grey Crags had begun to look much more like guide-book diagrams at last.

The first open groove to the heather terrace seems tricky, but succumbs to positive and dynamic bridging. The 1987 FRCC guide follows the 1949 edition in giving Spider Wall four pitches, but this is to break its 120ft (36m) up overmuch. With modern ropes it is logical and sensible to continue directly to the business of the crack.

The crack starts wide with decent footholds in front of you, but these soon run out. At 10ft (3m) the crack closes and it quickly becomes apparent that the only way to make progress is by lay-back. Above, the crucial handhold beckons, but the only foothold is away and up to the right. I was cocooned in slings but after the flared crack and another good wire beside the handhold, there was no protection until I had made that big bridge. A curving crack above my head came into reach then and, by dint of curling round upon myself and reaching out and backwards, I got another good nut seated here. When David Webster led it for my camera some weeks later, the niche was green and slimy and he was more than happy to find this placement, even though the top of the pinnacle is just to the left, together with a stonking belay.

My ropes ran straight down to Sally, 60ft (18m) below; her pale upturned face trusted me to hold her tight on the strenuous move. As she climbed, I looked down into the golden bowl of the coombe and thought how much a climb is enhanced by research – all that 'armchair mountaineering' we do in guides and journals, memoirs and accounts. Just like the ropes that hold us together on the climb, words are the threads of memory and experience, linking us to all our yesterdays. Down the years, this little piece of rock has absorbed the best efforts of some of the best rock climbers of a generation: I'm sure it intensifies the pleasures we can get out of the rock to remember their recorded thoughts as we repeat the climb.

The second pitch starts with steep and awkward steps up the groove on the right. Above, 40ft (12m) of open balance climbing lead to the top. The master feature of this slab is the thread-like seams which pattern the clean grey rhyolite. Thin and barely visible in places (while in others moss-filled and blank), they lead the unsuspecting climber to the centre of the web, the bracket. Here's Bill's account of why the climb was named the Spider's Wall: 'Once on the bracket the

John Baker preparing to step onto the bracket, pitch two, Spider Wall

(left) David Webster and John Baker at grips with the first pitch of Spider Wall

Sally Noble following John Baker onto the bracket

notion of the spider's web becomes apparent but whether one imagines oneself as the spider or the fly is purely a matter of existing form.'

There is little in the way of protection hereabouts, apart from some small nuts, so the balance onto the rounded edge of the bracket sets the ropes trembling like gossamer behind you. The grey rock throws the coloured life lines into high relief, which is just what you feel when you have made the next two moves and found a decent nut before the final steepness. My runners rattled hollowly; one tinkled back to Sally. Once again, I kept red tight until she was just about to make each move. The reassuring tension helped her own up to her fears in the middle of the web. She calmed and faced the crux. The ropes thrummed with her life and then went slack, thrummed and slackened, as she climbed purposefully up towards me and the future. In David Craig's words:

> *. . . The last fraction*
> *Of precarious poise is the first second*
> *Of the next rising. You cannot grasp the point*
> *Until you act on it, make it yours.*

A LICTOR'S LAMENT

Fortiter (4b), Grey Crag (W. Peascod and S. B. Beck, July 1941)

Fat climbers are a menace, but a limited amount of overweight might perhaps not inhibit well-trained men at the start of a relatively easy ascent.

(*The Seventh Grade*, Reinhold Messner)

'Don't touch that sausage, Tim!'

I paused in the breakfast-making and turned to frown at the speaker. David Webster was busily eating a bowl of prunes while John Baker was concentratedly pushing his muesli around, trying to get it under the milk and baby-food-soft.

'And why not, pray?' I enquired of them both.

'Because you're fat enough already and you aren't using up nearly as much energy as you ought to be doing by climbing all these rubbishy little routes. Why aren't you writing about 27 E3 climbs?' Dave replied from a full mouth, spitting prune stones into John's muesli.

I nearly threw the sausage at him. 'Because I'm not strong enough,' I answered, turning back to look sorrowfully at the rapidly shrinking length of Cumberland sausage.

'Precisely; it proves my point,' Dave savagely retorted in his best, no-nonsense new-wave, computer dealer's style.

Ever since he and John had decided it was time for a RURC – a Realised Ultimate Rock Climb – and started serious training for the Eiger, climbing with them (even being with them) had become almost intolerable. They had been converted to the John Barry gung-ho school of climbing: compulsory PT in the mornings followed by long runs before breakfast. Dave was even attempting to emulate St Reinhold by training his kidneys to cope with 'fluid deprivation'. 'No juice for me, thanks,' he would say after an hour or so's stiff walking uphill, 'I'm squeezing my filters dry.' Revolting! I sat down and ate the sausage loudly and very self-righteously. I knew I would need every calorie I could muster for the long day out in Birkness Coombe.

But before we could get out on the hill, I had to attend an Eiger gear selection session in Fisher's that lasted half the morning. Typically, The Team bought nothing for the RURC except some laces. Apparently, big plans don't go so well with chronic insolvency. More wasted time. Anyway, after they had made the most of a greasy Spider's Wall for lunch under the cameras, I marshalled the troops for another photo session on Fortiter, issuing orders and instructions in my best authoritarian style. I thought I would show them who was still the boss out on the hill.

'Sally and I did this little route a few weeks ago, but I'd just like to get a better photo if I can, so here's the plan. I'll go off and set up the abseil; give me fifteen minutes and then start to climb – slowly! Dave will be in the lead, dressed in the sky blue jacket. Everything clear?' I started to scramble off to the top of Chockstone Buttress and the abseil down Fortiter, calmly ignoring the sullen attitudes, the muttered impreca-tions and the not-so-muttered literary references like 'Fascist pig' and 'Squealer'. In fact, it was pleasing to see that John had remembered something of my teaching from *Animal Farm*.

From the abseil, though, things looked bad. First, I could see a vast grey cloud gathering over Borrowdale, blotting out Honister Pass; and second, a mutinous huddle of climbers under a boulder. The ropes were nowhere in sight. I decided bitter scorn was the best rousing tactic and addressed them in a hectoring tone from somewhere on Suaviter.

'Call yourselves alpinists,' I opened with, 'real alpinists would be thinking of climbing this in boots with sacks on. It's only 4b and the overhang is easy.' Silence. Now for the humiliation tack. 'Sally climbed it with me last week in ten minutes; I bet you'll take longer.' Silence. I was getting anxious. The light was fading fast. 'Look,' I shouted down eventually in exasperation, while trying desperately to remember all the Latin I had learned in 2x before I was demoted to the modern language set. '"Fortiter" means something to do with strength and I know you're really strong boys.' I was counting on hooking Dave's vain spot – he spends days of his life in one of those torrid gyms which are full of grunting, narcissistic anorexics and which stink of sweat and steel and Brut aftershave. It worked! John stopped kissing Joanna and lazily started uncoiling the rope while Dave got out the gear. There might just be enough time to get a picture before the light faded completely. I reviewed the sections of the climb through the lens.

There was the sharp start to get to the ledge

and nominally the end of the first pitch of 20ft (6m). If they got on the route before the light failed, I knew Dave would do it all in one full rope length of 150ft (45m). The crack follows, full of good holds, all the way to the overhang. From below this looks rather hard: the crack widens and is displaced by 3ft (1m) to the right. Blocky, square-cut overhangs appear to prevent access to the upper corner. But I remembered the beautiful move right to get into the crack on fantastic holds – rather like the crux of Blanco on Castle Helen at Gogarth, but much easier.

I could see the upper crack really well through the 50mm lens. The curious horizontal striations of this part of Grey Wall came out clearly. Swinging the camera down, I picked out Dave halfway up the crack. He was scowling. 'This thing is really wet and slippery, Tim,' he spat at me through clenched teeth.

'I know,' I called back, concentrating on focusing on his lime green and black check

harness, 'that's why you're climbing it now, in practice for a verglassed Hinterstoisser Traverse.' Things were going well; I clicked away.

Dave seemed unhappy all the way, but made the crux move look easy with his huge arm muscles hardly stretched and then ran up the easy final crack just ahead of the snow. John had to climb it to bring up Dave's waterproof and extra top, so he had the satisfaction of scoring off me when he pulled over in less than ten minutes wearing trainers and not much else in the pouring rain. 'There, that's about the only overweight that I shall be this season,' he said pointedly, looking at my waist and swinging off his bulky sack. 'We alpinists know that every

extra pound means wasted strength. Carrying rucksacks on climbs is one thing, paunches quite another. People who allow themselves to get plump should be dealt with most severely,' he added, warming to his theme until a very un-Roman thought struck him: 'Oh dear,' he suddenly exclaimed, barely concealing his delight, 'we won't be able to do Dexter Wall now, will we, because of this sleet? And you won't be able to drive us any further up the hill; so put your cane away and let's go home for tea.'

I couldn't help but wail and gnash my teeth. All that way again to get a decent photograph of these three Grey Crag routes and once again the weather had prevented it. Somewhat embarrass-ingly, Dave was all fired up by now and into alpine overdrive. I could see the light fanatical begin to burn behind his eyes. 'We *will* go on to the summit, sir,' he cried, 'if that's your wish.' John's response was just to giggle and disappear down into the mist hand in hand with Joanna. 'Oh, well; we tried. Brilliant little route though,' Dave said merrily as he once again refused my offer of a drink and set off at break-neck speed – his usual alpine descent rate.

And what about the Lictor, you may ask? Well, all I could do the whole way down to the car at Gatesgarth was lick the rain drips from my moustache and lament loudly.

ROMAN WALL BLUES

Dexter Wall (4b, 4c), Grey Crag (W. Peascod and S. B. Beck, March 1941)

When I'm a veteran with only one eye
I shall do nothing but look at the sky

('Roman Wall Blues', W. H. Auden)

You can see it from the valley, this wall of perfect rock, so smooth and clean-cut in the early morning sun that it is almost possible to believe it has been built to stop keen climbers in their tracks. Dexter Wall, neat partner to Buckstone Howe's Sinister Grooves, and the 'crowning classic' of Grey Crag, is a one-pitch route nowadays; but the belay ledge on the very edge of the Buttress provides a second with the perfect view of how to climb the crux and should not be missed.

Dexter Wall was one of the very few new climbs Bill inspected on a top rope first: 'To provide a top rope was so easy, and the wall especially near the upper edge, seemed so bare we decided that on this occasion, a little prudence could be profitable.' No doubt but that he would have had to clean the crucial crack and look to see if he could get a sling on before the crux. In the photograph of Bill and Bert on that first ascent it looks as if Bill found a runner on the big blunt spike which points the way from the traverse to the thin crack. Bert looks on patiently at a dynamic Peascod who is reaching up to the bottom of the crack. Even after top-rope inspection, it obviously wasn't easy. Bill records that 'on this stance, Bert stood for over an hour whilst I attempted the final crack.' Things haven't changed much today.

Sally stood patiently while I contemplated the moves up the crack. The protection is superb; the crack offers a perfect fit for modern nuts and Friends. But that is not the problem: it is the sequence of the holds. We had marched in double quick time up the first wide crack to the ledge, but now I couldn't work out how I was to stay on the wall.

Straight as a Roman road, bending slightly left at the top and almost disappearing, the crack goes, with slight edges either side of it for feet. Dexter, sinister, dexter, sinister; the legion's marching refrain rang in my ears. Could I really use those little edges either side while finger locking in the crack? On a closer inspection, I could see a swathe of cleared ground two feet either side of the crack, the evidence of other ascents.

Sally was standing sentinel-still on her stance, stoical in the cold wind as I reached inquisitively into the tiny niche at the start of the difficulties. It is so snug and perfectly formed, it feels as if it might once have held a votive offering. I swung up to reach the finger jams.

Nigel Birtwell and Christine Pearson complete the crux pitch of Dexter Wall, Grey Crag, at sunset

The Red Pike/High Stile ridge from Dexter Wall, showing the central Lakeland Fells in the distance

Nigel Birtwell on the lower section of Dexter Wall

Don't be misled by Bill Birkett's account of this pitch in the March 1986 edition of *Climber*. He says the wall 'keeps moving right, never really seeming to get exposed', but his photo of Cynthia Grindley perched above a long drop shows what it really feels like up here. This is no pleasant resting place; even if you are bridged off the spillikin with the left foot in a reasonable hold, it is a steep and lonely place. But no one can come and talk you out of the strain here, so you must cam and torque your own way up the wall, alone. It isn't very far, so grit your teeth and try to pacify the warring tribes of thoughts and feelings.

The crux is right at the top, just after you have committed all your force into the crack. The handholds close off and you must search up and left to find the weakness that will allow a final pull. From the top, if you're lucky, if the light is right and if you walk a little further west, you may be vouchsafed a view of where that real Roman wall, Hadrian's folly, starts in the Solway Firth.

Bill Peascod repeated Dexter Wall with David Craig in 1982, forty-one years after the first ascent. Unlike the typical Roman centurion, veteran of the wall, who would be pensioned off on a farm in some sunny clime to while away the hours and watch the sky, Bill kept on climbing, serving out his time, doing what he could do well. As David Craig writes, men like that are the true veterans, 'natural climbers/Working in the grain of rock' all their lives. We do well to follow where they lead.

The Walk from Grey Crag to Eagle Crag

After Dexter Wall, walk around the ridge to the slight col at the head of a broad scree gully which bounds the western end of the crag. This is the descent to Eagle Front. Leave the sacks here, or on the plateau at the top of the climb.

STEALING FIRE

*Eagle Front (4c, 4c, 4c, 4b, 4b), Eagle Crag
(W. Peascod and S. B. Beck, June 1940)*

Urizen explor'd his dens,
Mountain, moor and wilderness,
With a globe of fire lighting his journey.

('The Book of Urizen', William Blake)

Eagle Front is now a famous climb. Every VS leader seems to want to come up to Eagle nowadays to have a look at what is arguably Bill Peascod's most significant route in the Lakes. On good days, there is usually a skein of brightly coloured ropes and climbers on every pitch and stance and then the climb looks well stitched up. But when the rain clouds have been draped over the coombe for days, Eagle Crag becomes a different proposition and the numbers of aspirants to Eagle Front diminishes in direct proportion to the depth of slime on the first holds.

Bill's own ascents of this route are well documented in FRCC journals, his autobiography, *Journey After Dawn*, and *Native Stones*. But it is the Border television film of him climbing Eagle Front in socks, in his sixties, that did most to reintroduce him on his return from half a lifetime in Australia. At the first public showing of this film at the 1985 Kendal film festival, I well remember the gales of laughter and huge applause the down-to-earth Peascod elicited for his commentary about the condition of the climb and his own performance. His no-nonsense style and wholly unambiguous language *in extremis* rang a chord with every one watching. Here was a man, we realised, who was not afraid to repeat a route which, by all the rules, ought to have been quite beyond his powers. And because it almost was, he rose magnificently to the challenge. At the end of the film, the audience spontaneously rose to him, recognising perhaps that they had been watching one of the titans of the past, returned for an age to bring us all a sharper perspective on the sport

The crux overlap of Eagle Front, Eagle Crag. Nigel Birtwell and Christine Pearson the climbers

---

Looking down on Eagle Crag from Grey Crag. The Robinson Cairn path to Pillar is clearly seen just above the Red Pike ridge. Pillar itself is visible above the obvious gully leading up past Eagle Crag

so that we might the better understand the present. But it was not to be. He died in May 1985 on Cloggy, climbing, his new life stopped too soon, 'sucked down/Into the eating earth' where he had started, underground.

Bill's journey out of the mines into the freedom of the hills and air, to climb and paint, is William Blake's poetic journey in reverse. Here is a journey not from innocence to experience but the reverse, lived out in the demanding contexts of brutal manual work, self-imposed exile from the place he loved and art. In the climbing, I think he found how he could combine and reconcile these powerful, opposing forces.

I first climbed Eagle Front ten years ago with Sally. It was a day's flying visit from Lancaster where I had been bogged down in deadly lectures, essays and piles of books. I was half way to fulfilling an ambition to climb all the finest VS routes in Lakeland, going anticlockwise around the Lakes. That ambition is now fulfilled, but then, Buttermere was like another country, some new-found land.

Birkness Coombe was empty, I remember well. Our curious calls to each other across the air rebounded off the crags, splintering into the scree and startling sheep. There was no worn patch at the foot of the first pitch as there is today and everything was dry. We climbed as one without a pause or hint of difficulty, Sally leading the hardest move on pitch three. It was a day out of days, almost great. We were fuelled by love and deep desire for each other and the hills, all fired up with everywhere to go. It seemed unlikely life would ever be the same again.

In September 1988, working madly once again to write, I needed either to attempt another brilliant Peascod route on Eagle Crag – Fifth Avenue and Central Chimney – or to go back to Eagle Front. All summer I had been walking up into the coombe to look and see if Central Chimney could be climbed; all summer it had continued to drip. So I turned back to that wandering line that is perhaps the best expression of that exploring miner's eye for a line, Eagle Front. Dr Nigel Birtwell and Christine Pearson joined me for the day as part of their journey of exploration round the Lakes and love.

The route was only just in condition. The opening rib and groove were damp and covered in a dark green slime that reminded me of Pillar Rock. I had forgotten about the delicacy of a couple of the moves up the ramp on the second pitch, where the peg runner appears. The footholds are only just enough to balance on, especially when they're damp; and I held my breath as I moved cautiously into the steep little corner and rounded rib at the end of the traverse. Nigel had slipped momentarily here as he swung boldly up on rounded handholds, but had recovered instantly, an amazing feat considering what he was hanging from. Both Christine and I watched keenly as he described how best to overcome 'The Difficult Bit' as the FRCC 1987 guide calls it, and avoid the damp. Disconcertingly, the last runner is some way back, although that didn't affect us with top ropes.

This groove ends the difficulties of that long 100ft (30m) second pitch. But there is still a significant leftwards movement to be made across mossy slabs and gravel-covered holds before a further rightwards traverse on huge flakes leads to a little ledge below a bulge. Good double-rope technique is essential on this last pitch if a leader is going to prevent rope drag and offer realistic protection for a second. For Bill Peascod, this lead into the heart of Eagle up unknown ground, 'proved to be the most exacting of the climb'. Protection in the Forties consisted of a few heavyweight rope slings – not the easiest of things to deploy in thin cracks. Bill managed 'to get one in position on the gangway', but 'it was made of thick rope and it came off before he got to the top of the pitch'. I dare say there are a few leaders today who could manage that pitch without a runner, but the story should be read in the context of the day. In 1940 there was only a handful of climbers capable of leading at this grade, let alone leading new routes with minimal protection. Although the half century since then has taught us much more about the sort of rock that can be climbed and the training needed to climb it, it has taught us nothing new about the sort of courage that Bill Peascod showed then on Eagle Front.

I suppose the next pitch has the hardest technical move of the climb, but it is immediately above a good stance. Nigel, who is short, bridged from the obvious rounded hold on the left and swung up no-holds into the scoop. Christine did the same. When I stood up to it, I could reach the foothold with ease but could not believe the handholds underneath my nose. This move is a stopper on the best of days. I have seen huge queues build up here as frustrated leaders heave and haul, then swap around with their seconds. It's the sort of place where modern teams may still revert to that veteran dodge, the shoulder. But if you're tall enough, try reaching the good flake over to the right and pulling up the thickest bit of the bulge like I did then. It is fierce and painful, but at least the handhold is good.

Christine Pearson belaying Nigel Birtwell as he tackles the 4c moves of pitch five of Eagle Front

Above this test, some nasty scoops and awkward moves on broken rock lead to the terrace and, eventually, after a long walk left a peg belay on an excellent slab. Above, is the third 4c pitch – pitch five. Steep climbing up a cracked and jointed wall on sloping holds leads into an open groove and traverse right. Once again the protection is awkward to arrange in the thin cracks. The traverse eases slightly and leads in time to Nail Ledge. This exposed stance is now provided with good pegs to belay on; but Bill had only a 6in (15cm) nail from the pit to use, banged in with a stone. The stub is still on view, the prime exhibit of this big museum of cliff.

Nigel had carried on to the foot of the final pitch, effectively preventing me from photographing the traverse of pitch six. This is only given 4b but is quite the most intimidating of the lot. Wedged between the overhangs above and the deep green void below, it is thin and technical and damp. This would be the place to pin a titan down while the crag, the black bulk of Eagle, tears at the vitals, collecting more fears in its dripping bag of evidence.

The final moves on black slime in the water-worn groove were at my limit, panic almost setting in. Eagle Front, we should remind ourselves, in anything except the dry is a serious climb. Even Nigel acknowledged that he had felt 'liverish', dry-mouthed, almost dehydrated on these last moves – not, apparently, so much because they were sopping wet, but because they were compact and friable and runnerless. Bill, too, had pause for thought it seems: 'I discovered just how delicate this traverse was and pondered on the sloping nature of the holds and what they would be like in wet weather.'

And all that's left is the crack. This crack can be seen from beside the Lake, a great cleaved corner crack that looks really hard. In fact, it is about Severe, liberally supplied with holds and provides you with an exercise in corner climbing that never taxes, but never dulls. At the top, I moved onto the right wall and inadvertently knocked off a little rock. It flew down the corner striking sparks from the sharp-edged crack, then spun out into space and tinkled impotently 500ft (152m) below on the scree. The image stayed with me as we coiled the ropes and waded contentedly up onto the ridge. We were met by a blue and empty heaven, the giant peaks of central Lakeland etched darkly on the backcloth of the sky and a sunset that drove the cold from our limbs. Standing with my friends in that light was transforming. What I felt was something more than evening sun or friendship – it was more like the sparks that falling stones can make and related to the climb itself.

As we journeyed around the rim of Birkness Coombe to dawdle up Dexter Wall in the dusk, I remembered Bill's words about his feelings after climbing Eagle Front. For Bill it had been one of those days of days when he and Bert had stolen something precious out of time. He was to spend the next thirty years abroad unconsciously learning how to paint back the experience of those days and climbs in Buttermere by fusing his oils with fire. Coming from the underworld into the mountains and the light, he found the right Promethean fire itself, stolen when the gods had turned their backs. After Eagle Front, nothing was ever quite the same again.

We sat there together, in the sun. The evening was still; we were completely alone in the coombe – in the World! The War, the pit . . . they didn't exist. We didn't say much. What was there to say? Each of us was drenched in his own emotions, dreaming his own dreams . . .

The Walk from Eagle Crag to Buttermere

The broad ridge to the summit of High Crag provides one of the most dramatic views in Lakeland: full in the south, Scafell lords it over a knot of peaks. If it is late in the afternoon, the sun will be full on these mountains. And across Ennerdale the high level route to Pillar will also be clear.
Carry on down the ridge to Scarth Gap and turn towards Buttermere once again.

Nigel Birtwell powering up the final crack of Eagle Front

7 E·N·N·E·R·D·A·L·E

The Walk from Wasdale Head Hotel to Pillar Rock

The only route to Pillar is from Wasdale, the route the first explorers of the rock took a hundred years ago. Although the rock can be approached from High Gillerthwaite in Ennerdale or from Buttermere as Oppenheimer sometimes did, the finest – perhaps the finest path in Lakeland – contours round the broken slopes of the Pillar massif to Robinson's Cairn and Pillar Cove. This path is almost alpine in its rugged grandeur; and although this approach is much longer than any other (almost two hours when you are carrying equipment), the views more than make up for the time.

It goes without saying that a very early start is necessary if the best part of the day is to be spent on the cliff. Indeed, if the weather is kind and you carry on from Grooved Wall to try Gomorrah and the Girdle, expect a late return.

Turn left at the Wasdale Head Hotel and strike up the slowly rising path to Black Sail Pass. After crossing the Gatherstone Beck, the pass swings almost east to reach the col. Before it does, leave it and climb steeply up the back of the coombe to the col left of point 627. A little higher, on the northern side, a steep little gully leads down to the faint high path to Hind Cove. Keep on the top path all the way until it meets the broader path below in Hind Cove. Robinson's Cairn is on the point of the next spur and is the first sight of the rock. Make for the blue stretcher box below Shamrock. The foot of Grooved Wall is 55yd (50m) away to the right of Walker's Gully. It is probably worth carrying a small pouch containing water if you intend to be climbing for several hours; but sacks will be safe at the foot of the climb. The descent from Pillar is notoriously difficult, especially in the mist, so real study of the FRCC guide-book is advised. The long scree ramp which returns eastwards to the foot of Shamrock will eventually be followed and then it is a simple matter to retrace your steps back along the path to Robinson's Cairn and Black Sail Pass.

MARKINGS

Grooved Wall (4b, 5a, 4b, 4c), North Face of Low Man, Pillar Rock (H. M. Kelly, H. G. Knight and W. G. Standring, April 1928)

The longest journey is the journey inwards.

(*Markings*, Dag Hammarsköld)

Sometimes you travel hopefully but don't want to arrive. The journey to Pillar via Hopkinson's Cairn on a wet and misty day is just like that. As the dark North face of Low Man comes into sight with the towers of the summit skirling in a shroud of cloud, the heart drops. It doesn't need the overlaid sound of rushing water, carried on the pulsing current of wind around the coombe to make you realise that the cliff is dripping, green and slimy; you can see it from the cairn, looking like a Hammer horror set, gaunt and haunted, dark as the grave.

One week in August, Terry Gifford and I spent five frustrating days at Joss Naylor's farm at Bowderdale in Wasdale, watching the curtains of rain draw across the screes and Joss shearing his oily sheep by hand under a single bulb. For months we had been waiting to try the Pillar Girdle, the longest route of its kind in England, but conditions were never good enough. I was reduced to quoting from Oppenheimer's *Heart of Lakeland* to keep our spirits up: 'Happily the finest Lakeland climbs are all out of the way on the hill-tops, and the tramps to them are delightful preludes to the climbs, amongst which none are finer or more varied than that . . . to Pillar.'

One hopeful foray, from a very early start, turned into a filthy struggle up North climb in a down-pour when I rationalised the climb by quoting the Pillar pioneers who had climbed up in any conditions. But how had they done it? As

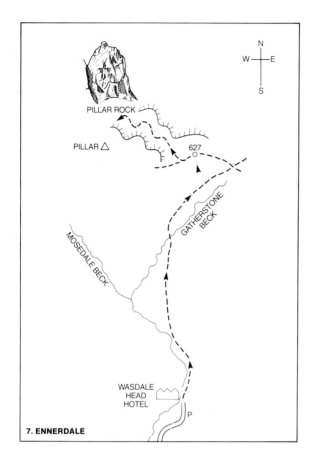

7. ENNERDALE

Labels on map: PILLAR ROCK · PILLAR △ · 627 · MOSEDALE BECK · GATHERSTONE BECK · WASDALE HEAD HOTEL · P · N W E S

But the ledges above the last groove are turf-covered and when the waters sluice down the face, the cracks choke up. Lots of dry days will be required before the crux move can be overcome and the last steep groove be bridged cleanly.

Before the first ascent, Kelly had to clean the intervening groove carefully – all 120ft (36m) of it. His diary for 26 April 1928 records 'Extensive grubbing' in the long groove, enough to make it look 'presentable'. I can see him fussing over the pitch like a parent over a recalcitrant child. Given the slight angle outwards of parts of this pitch and the equipment of the time, I imagine they had some exciting moments. However, on the 26th, neither Kelly nor Knight could lead the lower overhang which is the crux; 5½ hours' hard labour was wasted. Two days later they returned and 'Standring spent 2½ hours giving the long Groove and the ledges below a final sweep up'. In total, they put in a day of cleaning and gardening, most of it from a top rope – a thoroughly modern approach. Kelly records that they sent enough earth down into Ennerdale 'to

one of the highest crags in the Lakes and the closest to the sea, the rock soon gets covered in a particularly odious slime which fills the pocketed rock and makes friction a rare commodity. I began to realise that I might have to settle for an attenuated plan: we would go up known ground on Grooved Wall and round to Gomorrah on the big West Face. Here at any rate are two of the finest VS climbs in the Lakes in a magnificent setting, and both the product of the founding father of modern rock climbing, Harry Kelly. If Gomorrah was climbable, so would be the Girdle. But as we know too well, some journeys never end.

Grooved Wall is Kelly's hardest climb on Pillar and, together with Tophet Bastion and Moss Ghyll Grooves, one of his finest creations. The line is obvious on the great hanging curtain of rock that falls into Walker's Gully, a series of hanging ramps, formed obviously by a sheet of rock ripping away. By all the physical laws of the universe, the steepness of the wall and the angle of the ramps should ensure that they are protected from infestation with earth and moss.

The author on the way to Pillar in the rain (Terry Gifford)

provide soil for the whole of the re-afforestation scheme'. Such a mark he made on the cliff to last for years, and he knew it would.

Charlie Davis, Pete Clarke and I came up to photograph the climb in September. It was like a morgue, but Charlie cheerfully geared up and, with cagoule flapping eccentrically, sluiced up the opening chimney. Wedged in the wide trough, feet scything swathes of grot off the flake, he confessed to feeling scared. The first real open climbing follows up a groove, curving to the left slightly. Mist was swirling in again from the north as I jigged and paced around trying to keep warm. Pete was hunched inside his cagoule, his flat cap constructing an illusion of warmth. I realised that we were going nowhere like this: Charlie had recently been repeating some modern desperates in Huntsman's Leap, but had slowed to a crawl on this VS as he redug his way up the groove. Suddenly, a huge screech rent the air. The echoes swept around the chamber of Walker's Gully like a banshee host. 'Aaaargh! that was bloody desperate,' Charlie shrieked, pulling onto the slippery ledge below the crux overhang. And then, in a more normal voice; 'It's obvious how to do it; I swear I can see old nailmarks on the rib.' Pete didn't move, but the clouds did, and he disappeared from sight. For another hour I stood and cursed as they struggled with the climb. The rope that was being trailed for me writhed and twisted on itself in the dank vegetation, mute testament to the anguish above.

Charlie waited for Pete to refix some nuts in apposition and then, in a masterly show of climbing, bridged up the crux overhang. There is a thin flared crack in the wall in front of you (but it offers nothing positive) and good lay-back holds running down the overhang (but there is nothing much for the feet). Like the CB lay-back (which Kelly tried once and then never again), it gets harder the higher you go; and you know that disingenuous words like 'effect a lodgement in the groove above' is guide-book speak for 'this will be at your technical limit'. It is perilously easy to get hold of the high lay-backs and find yourself with feet level with hands but with nothing to reach across for to pull them over the

yawning gap. I couldn't see how Charlie had bridged it, but it worked.

For another 100ft (30m) the groove rises up the wall – mostly straightforward, well-protected bridging and dynamic weight changes past a good belay to a steepness. The position here is breathtaking. The retaining wall crowds you and the slightly out-of-balance move up feels very insecure. Above, the turf drips begin to feed the ledges and the stance below the final pitch is a patch of garden beside a block. Our shouts by now were all that kept us in touch. The red light in my camera lens didn't register on the scale. Pete's muffled curses came from the cloud but without a revelation. I wondered how they would get down.

The first moves of the final pitch are hard again, like the start of Dinas Mot Direct's last pitch. A good flat hold out on the edge of the flying rib looks useful but is too far away and the bulge is right in front. Pray there is no moisture here because you're more than a rope length from the ground, even if you would be swinging about over Walker's Gully. A crucial triangular pocket higher up enables another good flat hold on the edge to be reached and, by building bridges across the groove, the turf fields are reached at last.

Charlie and Dave elected to abseil rather than proceed with the rest. Their ropes dangled out of the cloud like some bizarre Indian fakir's trick while I scoffed all the remaining mints · and worried about the photographs. I'd spent over a day trying to get this route on film and time was running out. When the lads got down, they looked anything but presentable. Charlie's face was marked by streaks of mud and grime and Pete's hands looked as if he had been shovelling earth with them. 'One hell of a route; I was really frightened on the crux,' Charlie declared. 'Easier in the dry, of course,' he added looking for the mints. 'Did you get some decent photographs by the way? It was impossible up there to take a black and white.' I didn't answer. They stopped packing the sacks and looked questioningly at me, then hostilely at me. 'We're not coming back you know. That's it!'

But at nine the next morning after an hour's drive from Thirlmere and another huge walk we were in cloud again looking at the marks we had made the day before and were praying for some light and an end to journeying.

Charlie Davis and Pete Clarke complete pitch two of Grooved Wall, Pillar Rock, in desperate conditions

8 W·A·S·D·A·L·E

▌ *The Walk from Wasdale Head Hotel to Kern Knotts Crag*

The walk to Kern Knotts from the Wasdale Head Hotel, followed by the traverse of the Napes must be the most written about in the Lake District. These crags were the forcing grounds of the first Tigers, this traverse path their access. From the hotel, go east across a field to the tiny church – surely one of the most dramatic sites for worship in Britain – and then follow the good track to Burnthwaite Farm. Follow the broad path beyond over Gable Beck and take the obvious scree path which rises up and across the broad slopes of Great Gable. Kern Knotts Crag itself can be reached from this path by turning off just before a broken knoll, 100ft (30m) below the Sty Head Pass. An obvious scree fan and incipient path lead directly to the distinctive Sty Head face of the crag.

KEEPING UP WITH THE JONESES

Kern Knotts Crack (4b), Kern Knotts Crag (O. G. Jones and H. C. Bowen, April 1897)

'Well, Jones, if you climb that crack I'll never speak to you again!'

(John Robinson to O. G. Jones)

The little outcrop of Kern Knotts rests on the Gable Traverse like a tightly clenched fist. The Sty Head (east) face of the crag is split by two obvious cracks, the lines of two very fine climbs, Innominate and Kern Knotts Crack. Innominate fell in 1921 to the powerful and prolific Lakes climbers G. S. Bower and Bentley Beetham; but Kern Knotts Crack has a special place in Lakeland climbing history because in 1897, the year of its first ascent, only a handful of Lakeland climbs had been given the VS grade and because it is a product of that rock climbing genius, O. G. Jones.

Jones must have been something of a phenomenon to his contemporaries. A compulsive trainer and gymnast, he could perform the sort of feats on and off the rocks that other men could only dream of achieving. Oppenheimer's famous account of Jones's 'passage of the billiard table leg' in *The Heart Of Lakeland* and of his traverse of the billiard-room walls is bettered only by the Abraham tale of Jones lifting Abraham under his right arm and then doing three three-fingered pull-ups from a horizontal ice-axe.

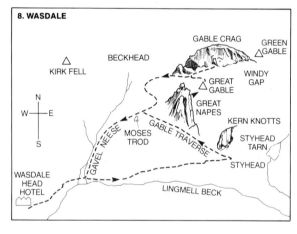

These exploits clearly show Jones to be the forerunner of the modern rock athlete. Certainly, the boldness of his explorations – often done solo and in marginal conditions – stands out clearly down the years. The quality of his routes is still apparent, too, and they bear comparison with the host of modern routes that surround them. It matters not the grade: a bold and obvious line will always be attractive to a rock climber with a discerning eye and sense of history.

Of all Jones's routes, though, perhaps Kern Knotts Crack epitomises his contribution to Lakeland climbing. Completed only after top rope inspection, the help of a judiciously placed ice-axe at the top of the sentry box and three attempts at the crux (where Jones found two wedged stones that forced his body 'out of the crack altogether'), it waited a year for him to lead it from the ground. His ascent must have opened every good climber's eyes to the host of possibilities in Wasdale alone. For Jones, of course, it eventually became a show case route on which he could demonstrate his considerable strength and skill. The story goes that Jones grew so expert at the moves that he could solo up the crack and down Kern Knotts Chimney in seven minutes. If that story is true, it is a feat one rarely sees repeated nowadays, although it is significant, because that is just the sort of competition you can find on any outcrop in the country today, where regulars attempt to impress a visitor with a show of power and strength on well-practised routes. But Kern Knotts Crack is still no push-over, and although it is by no means desperate by modern standards, it certainly qualifies for the status of 'Traditional Classic'.

For a climb to be accorded the accolade of 'Traditional Classic' it must surely fulfil the following criteria:

a It must have been climbed before World War I.
b It must be well polished.
c It must be awkward if not difficult to protect, even with modern equipment.
d It must be strenuous and/or technical and demanding of technique.
e It must follow a definite and 'inescapable' line.
f It must be hard enough to make even very good climbers think carefully.

On all these counts, Kern Knotts Crack scores highly. It is one of the very best short routes in the Lake District.

The weekend that I set off with Dr Nigel Birtwell, Sally and Christine to climb it for the third time was cold and raw. Snow lay like spilt sugar on Scafell and down as far as the Great Napes. The trek up the broad path to Sty Head was taken at break-neck speed as always, partly to get stiff muscles warmed up and partly to rekindle our competitive instinct. The seventeen years of friendship between the doctor and me is based as much on competition as on mutual admiration, affection and respect.

Three-quarters of an hour later, Christine and I found a safe and comfortable spot in the vile pile of broken boulders that have fallen from the Sepulchre area of Kern Knotts and started to tug on cold rock boots. 'What grade's the other crack?' the doctor demanded from a distance away.

'VS or thereabouts,' I called back as I beat my hands into life around my chest. Christine looked blue, even with three pullovers on. The wind was streaming round the Wasdale face, super-cooling the rock. I finished tightening my laces and looked up. The doctor was half-way up Innominate Crack. I remember Christine and myself staring at each other in semishock and feeling foolish. Almost before we had looked back at the crack, the doctor was up and out of sight. We were speechless with envy and disbelief. When he joined us ten minutes later, grinning like the proverbial Cheshire cat who has licked the cream, we both gave vent to our feelings loudly, accusing him of deliberately undermining our confidence. This outburst had absolutely no effect whatsoever.

'Look,' I said, borrowing one of his own preposterous linguistic constructions from his Leeds University Climbing Club days, 'I'm the Attitude Inspector and I think your attitude needs inspecting. I can't solo VS routes on cold days: how on earth do you think I can keep up with you? This is a day for sharing traditional routes.' But I might as well have kept quiet; he was already at the crux of Kern Knotts Crack giving a nonstop Chris Brasher-like commentary of the 'once-in-the-space-of-a-lifetime-comes-a-climber-such-as-this' type, at the same time as demonstrating Jones-like finger pull-ups on tiny holds. It was such a calculated and outrageous performance that we disregarded his momentary silence as he did a wide splits to climb the top of the sentry box because we knew that in this mood he was capable of grossly exaggerating any difficulty. Sure enough, with Olympian style, he monkeyed up the rest of the crack in three or four minutes.

There are two starts: the crack direct or a little wall on small edges to reach the ledge at the base of the sentry box. I had to follow the crack to retrieve Nigel's first (token) runner that was under the bulge on the left. The moves were steep and strenuous and needed a very quick and positive response.

A grasp for the smooth floor of the niche, a heave and rock over and I found myself looking up at the overhanging, converging walls of the niche/sentry box. Worse than the flared chimney of Demo Route at Sennen, it looked the stuff of nightmare. I stepped out onto the lines of edges on the face to the right and moved up to the limit of footholds. The last runner was a small wire in a tiny slot behind the stub of flake I was standing on with my right foot. I remembered the terror I had felt when I had first climbed this crack years ago on finding that my secret weapon, a huge hexentric nut, would not fit the crack. I still couldn't see how any modern equipment would fit in until after the crux move, although a possible thread is available above. The bridge is wide and on a nail-polished rounded, vertical edge in the crack. If the jammed stone wasn't there at just the right place, the move would be desperate. However, with a modicum of strength, confidence and technique it is over quickly. But hang around and look at it too long in a cold wind and you will begin to feel how that select band of climbers at the Wasdale Head must have felt in the late 1890s: that there's no keeping up with the Joneses of the climbing world.

Above the niche, the crack is wide but climbable by holds on either edge. Resist the temptation to get wedged into its dank depths, though: that way despair lies. If you look carefully, there are just sufficient little finger nicks to help you avoid the antique polish of the crack sides.

As I slapped the top holds, nearly pausing to gaze admiringly at my reflection in them, the doctor suggested that, to speed things up, he should lower me on the belay plate. I looked at his pawky smile and, without a word, still looking him straight in the eye, leaned out backwards as if on abseil. He lowered me like a sack of potatoes to the bottom. Christine fared the same after she had fought her way up with frozen hands – except that she received a kiss as well. By the time we had coiled the ropes, the doctor was round the base of the crag again, still cheerful, despite the fact that he must have been frozen, and asking what was next and was it really challenging. 'You don't beat the mountain, you beat yourself,' I told him primly, trying to reassert the good old romantic values of the sport while privately wondering if he had taken less than five minutes to get down Kern Knotts Chimney.

'No, it's the move! The move you make,' he retorted. 'You beat the mountain with the move – and by the way, that crux move was harder and better than anything on Innominate: good VS, I thought.' He was sitting on his sack, drinking orange juice, so, hoping to steal a march on him, I suggested that Christine, Sally and myself should set off for the Napes and let out gallant leader catch us up. 'To rest is not to conquer,' I called back to him over my shoulder and then watched, dumbfounded, as, less than ten minutes later, he came running into the lead on the Gable Traverse.

'Are you resting, Tim, or just trying to beat yourself?' he called out cheekily as he sped past. Trying to keep up with him all the way to the Napes, I understood why John Robinson had threatened never to speak to Jones again.

The Walk from Kern Knotts Crag to Great Napes and Gable Crag

If returning to the base of Kern Knotts is a test piece of down-climbing, the continuation of the walk to the foot of Eagle's Nest Ridge also contains a challenge: the threading of Napes Needle. A path well below the broken ridge from which the Needle rises can be traversed, followed by a steep, unpleasant and even dangerous ascent of Needle Gully. It is better, though, to scramble up to the gap between the Needle and Needle Ridge and down-climb the other side. A rope may be useful for nervous members of the party.

The Dress Circle, a little rock-encircled green oasis is just beyond the gully. It is imperative that sacks be carried on this climb, otherwise an expensive descent from the summit of the ridge will be necessary, followed by a long traverse to White Napes and a walk round the western slopes of Great Gable to the foot of Sledgate Ridge. Reach the summit of Gable instead by the Westmorland Crags route. From the summit go directly north down a broken scree slope to an obvious V-groove with a huge block at its top. This is the top of Engineer's Slabs. Either abseil down the route from here (not really fair, of course, because you will see that phenomenal last pitch), or leave the sacks and gain the base of the climb by following the main path from Gable Summit north-east, almost to Windy Gap. A climber's traverse leads back to the steep little wall of Sledgate Ridge. Consult the FRCC Gable Guide if you don't want to use this ridge as an approach to Engineer's Slabs.

Nigel Birtwell bridges the crux of Kern Knotts Crack

VICTORIAN VALUES

Eagle's Nest Ridge Direct (4b), Napes (G. A. Solly, W. C. Slingsby and party, April 1892)

To strive, to seek, to find, and not to yield

('Ulysees', Tennyson)

On a cold day in April 1892, Godfrey Solly led Cecil Slingsby and two others up the finest and hardest of the Napes ridges. Eagle's Nest Ridge Direct, as he called it, was the first British rock climb to be given the VS grade – a grade it still retains to this day, albeit in the slightly reduced form of Mild VS.

Solly's account of the climb (quoted by Alan Hankinson in *The First Tigers*), frankly admits to combined tactics to get off the first platform – the 'eagle's nest' itself; difficulty of communication with the rest of the party; an uninviting retreat from above the second step and, reading between the last, self-effacing lines, a technical crux more or less at the top.

The climb was apparently considered so serious as to be almost unwarrantable. Jones declared that '. . . the ridge is not to be recommended', and Solly himself, in all modesty and without a hint of contemporary, self-inflating irony, left advice on record that because the 'margin of safety' on the climb 'was so narrow . . . no-one should climb it unless he had previously reconnoitred it with a rope from above'. Today, such an account would be the equivalent of an open invitation to attempt a repeat ascent; but, according to Hankinson, some of these Victorian gentlemen climbers genuinely believed that publication of the details of 'dangerous climbs' would only lead to 'the young and the foolhardy' attempting climbs way beyond their ability, thus courting disaster.

The debate about publication of details of climbs, in Britain at least, is long resolved and nobody now would claim that Eagle's Nest Ridge is a 'dangerous climb'. But it is worth remembering, as we slot a small nut behind the tiny flake before the crux, that Solly was making these moves with cold hands, in nailed boots, with hemp rope, no runners and little prospect of retreat.

The strengths of character that a man like Solly exemplified on Eagle's Nest Ridge are for Alan Hankinson precisely the qualities of the 'Victorian middle-class English gentleman'. But the values and qualities of 'sturdy independence . . . abounding energy, curiosity and thoroughness' that these men espoused and displayed are, Hankinson claims, no longer fashionable in the late twentieth century; and, in a telling line, perhaps hinting at our modern style of petulant and youthful braggadocio, he maintains that 'the greatest crime for them would be to be caught bragging'. Now, whether we agree with these assertions or not, it is impossible not to feel admiration for Solly's modest account of the first ascent of the ridge and his courage in the lead. If we really need to look back to the beginnings of the sport of rock climbing in order to clarify our views about competitive climbing today, then surely the Victorian values we can respect are best represented by this lead into the difficult unknown. Solly led the ridge on sight, without an abseil inspection.

Certainly, it was partly the historical and cultural significance of the climb that led me to include it in this book. But it was also my own admiration for Solly's achievement and my near hero-worship of Slingsby that prompted me to set out to climb the ridge on a cold April day, a week before the ninety-sixth anniversary of the first ascent, determined to do without a runner on the full 120ft (36m) run out. If Solly had done without, so could I, I reasoned, especially since I would probably be climbing in sticky boots. In the event, however, things didn't work out as neatly as I had planned.

The ridge sweeps starkly up behind the Dress Circle, a natural balcony at the foot of Abbey Buttress. The name 'Dress Circle', like those other clever and amusing names for rock forms on Scafell, 'The Waiting Room' and 'The Fives Court', perfectly evokes the duality of these Victorian gentlemen's experiences in starched formality and exuberant play.

Easy steps lead up steep rocks to a ledge overlooking the Dress Circle. Above, the ridge narrows and steepens into a slight bulge, necessitating a pull around to the right and a large flake. When I had got there, climbing through a whetted wind, my fingers looked like deep-frozen sausages. Despite the fibre-pile jacket, my heart was icing up.

The thick twin cracks that rise above this ledge are the first real test of moral fibre. They look and feel oldfashioned: red and rugged inside but encrusted with small edges. Steep enough to require some muscle power in the jamming, they succumb easily enough to this technique coupled with wide bridging. As soon as possible, however, I pulled round onto the crest of the ridge proper and stepped up to the small square 'platform', the Eagle's Nest.

I didn't do what Solly did here and sit down, 'a leg dangling each side' of the ridge, but turned and rested against the rock. A mile or so across the arctic air of the upper dale, Great End and Scafell Pike froze in their diplomatic dance of flattery round lordly Scafell. The blustery up-draughts brought me distorted rumours of Lingmell Beck. My toes froze.

It is 15ft (4.5m) to the next pause, the Crow's Nest, and every foot is delicate. My lightweight ropes were beginning to waft in the wind, the gentle tugs at my waist intensifying as I balanced higher, still without a runner. But in a little scoop below a steepening where the holds ran out, the exposure and the cold were suddenly too much. I called back down to the doctor, Sally, Richard and Christine, but no one heard me against the wind. Perhaps they had gone round into hiding in Needle Gully to try to get warm. Trying to fish with frozen fingers for a small wire runner, I started to shiver violently. I was out over deep water again. And then a horrible thought struck me: what if nobody was holding the rope? Perhaps my bombastic boasting earlier about seeking the same experience as Solly and striving to emulate his achievement had been believed and they were letting me solo the ridge with a backrope.

After a brief bout of body bashing to summon up the blood, I looked for the sequence of pressure and balance holds at the crux. The carabiner on my runner, conducted by the wind, rang and tinkled against the iron rock in a sort of ghastly parody of a musical performance. Looking down, I still couldn't see anyone. I really did have cold feet and my hands would have looked perfect on one of Madame Tussaud's waxworks. What did Solly feel here? 'After looking around, something of a hold for each hand and foot was discovered, and I went on, with the knowledge that even if one hand or foot slipped, all would be over.' Well, I wasn't in that sort of fix, but the delicate balance up to the left followed by one right was sufficiently taxing in

the gusty wind to get me slightly gripped. Right on the edge, I balanced out of difficulty in a delightful sequence. It must have been terrifying in nails, though.

By the time that the doctor and Christine had arrived at the top of the pitch, so had the snow. No one wanted to climb the final little slab on the left on sloping holds to reach the easy part of the ridge and thus Gable summit by the Westmorland crags route; but also, no one wanted to call a halt, even though it was obvious to all that the day was drifting away from us. The doctor was purple with cold, Christine almost immobile and I was convinced that the warfarin I had been prescribed to thin my blood and prevent a recurrence of blood clots in the lungs was working in perfect harmony with the snow and wind, thus guaranteeing that my ears and nose would have to be amputated back at Wasdale Head.

Eventually, after I had declared that the game was up, even the indefatigable doctor, clad eccentrically for his ascent of the ridge in what looked like a moth-eaten Mongolian pixie's hat, demurred. I dropped a big sling around a miniature Napes Needle below the final slab and we slid down cold ropes to the comparative warmth of the Dress Circle.

It was only when we had bashed along the traverse to White Napes, sat down in a huddle and tried not to break our teeth on deep-frozen chocolate bars that the doctor nonchalantly raised the issue of the next route on Gable Crag. The prospect was unattractive: snow would be inches deep on the holds. But where was my fortitude, perseverance, courage, inspiration and leadership now, I wondered, as a bitter wind whirled a few snow flakes about us and cloud shrouded the crags. In similar conditions, those Victorian giants of a hundred years ago such as Solly and Slingsby, with frozen beards, ropes like hawsers and bags of insouciance, would probably have pressed on to the summit and perhaps another climb. But that was then, this was now, and we were all getting very cold again. Enough was enough: twentieth-century discretion ought to triumph over nineteenth-century valour. It was time to yield to the mountain weather, to seek the warmth of the hotel bar, to strive to get there just as they were starting to serve hot suppers and to live to climb on Great Gable another day.

MECHANISTIC MACHINATIONS

Engineer's Slabs (4c, 4c, 4c/5a), Gable Crag (F. R. Balcombe, J. A. Shepherd and C. J. A. Cooper, April 1934)

Engineer's Slabs must have been sparsely protected . . . whatever the nature of the engineering involved

(Paul Nunn, *Hard Rock* essay)

Because of its position and nature, this climb is one of the most taxing VS climbs in Lakeland. David Craig and Bill Peascod were lucky to climb it in fair condition one summer evening in 1984. I had hoped to repeat their experience – perhaps even climbing with David; but sadly, it was not to be. The letter which follows told David Craig what he'd missed!

Dear David,
Isn't the back of Gable an evil place? Oh yes, I know the crag is set in a magnificent position – almost as stunning as Scafell or Pillar, I suppose, and the rock is magnificent granite; but, like the North Face of the Eiger, it's often in cloud when everywhere else, including Gable summit itself, is in bright sunlight. You know, I'm not surprised that people rarely visit it: everything is dank and gloomy. And then there's the wind! If I tell you that last Sunday, the good Doctor Birtwell, Christine Pearson and I spent some six and a half hours in a half gale which was blowing remorselessly all the way up Ennerdale from the sea while we climbed Sledgate Ridge and Engineer's Slabs, I'm sure you'll appreciate my mixed feelings about the cliff.

Which brings me to the point. I bet your ascent of 'Balcombe's bombshell' (as Nigel christened it after leading the first two pitches in one and finding not much of a stance) with dear old Bill Peascod a few years back was an eye-opener for you both, wasn't it? I mean, it's not a slab at all, is it? Even Paul Nunn told us it wasn't a slab back in 1975: 'This wall is a "slab" only in name, for it is slightly convex, providing steep sustained

Nigel Birtwell balances up the crux of Eagle's Nest Ridge Direct, Great Napes, in bitterly cold conditions

climbing in a remote and unfrequented mountain environment.' Well, if that isn't a clear warning about a serious undertaking, I don't know what is. But you know the doctor: 'If it's got to be done, Tim,' he said to me on the phone, 'it's got to be done, hasn't it?' There really is no answer to that sort of rhetorical question is there? I merely nodded dumbly into the mouthpiece and looked out of the window at the driving rain. I forget, of course, that you've been in the far North where I daresay the weather has been reasonable; but down here in Wiltshire it's been abominable and every weekend in the Lakes the clouds have opened just as I've got the camera out.

I must tell you, I was frankly terrified about what we were going to find in that final flared groove – you know, the groove which Nunn helpfully warns us can retain winter verglass in dry spring weather, 'even when the rest of the climb is dry'. Images of this kept cropping up, Lady Macbeth-like in sleep. I started having nightmares of Nigel in a pair of thin green tights and a striped jersey bridged across a long smear of black ice, sobbing in the freezing air and totally committed without a runner. Melodramatic you might say, but in the event, not far off the reality, I can tell you.

Anyway, we did it . . . just. And I have to say that this must be one of the most serious VS climbs I've ever done – certainly the hardest one of the 27 I have selected for the book. Even if it had been completely dry (and I'll bet you at any odds, that that top groove will never be completely dry), the technical climbing, the steepness and the poor stances make it serious. Poor? I can hear you ask. Well, at one stage all three of us were standing on one foothold at the bottom of the lay-back crack, secured to four different nuts. And before you turn up your Constable or FRCC guidebook, I can tell you that yes, there are several stances mentioned in the pitch descriptions from the sentry box up ('sentry box'? what 'sentry box'?). I found two narrow pods with sloping floors separated by a fin of rock at the steepest point of the first pitch. The top one had a rusty old stub of a peg and one of Nigel's smallest wires as a runner.

I suppose I could have turned sideways and constructed a sort of belay in it, but it would have been one hell of a place to hold a fall, and out of sight of the leader in the top groove. Look

Nigel Birtwell on Engineer's Slabs pitch one

at the picture in *Hard Rock* again, and you'll see what I mean. Anyway, I could only just fit in, and I must be as big as a guardsman even without a rifle and bearskin. I still managed to make a mess of which hand to use on the sloping hold at the back while my shoulders had inadvertently jammed in the narrowing. Nigel saw me caressing the long sling he had left on the wire rather longingly and peremptorily issued an order to put it down at once. Perhaps that's what's meant by the sentry box.

Incidentally, thank God for Friends! I know you'll consider that a heresy, but it really came home to me on this climb that merely because I can climb VS doesn't mean to say I can really climb VS. I mean, Balcombe was up there in 1934 with hemp and probably no runners at all, wasn't he? Even with pegs for belays and short pitches, a fall out of that groove near the top would probably have been unstoppable and possibly fatal. You're absolutely right: some of our predecessors knew how to climb! But I wonder what you and Bill did for belays? Even the good ledge below the final groove had a poxy-looking peg and not much else. Did you find a hex placement in that big crack up to the left? You know, the one which is supposed to provide an alternative finish in case the groove is impossible. But I'm beginning to ramble, aren't I?

Sledgate Ridge is the perfect route to get to the base of the slab. We found it quite tricky in the damp, especially that stiff little opening wall. Nigel had led out all the rope (as usual) so it was impossible either to hear him or to shout instructions. At the top of the wall, I was just beginning to notice I had no feeling in my right hand when, hey presto! I was suddenly landing slap on me soles, back on the ground. Much merriment all round, including, surprisingly, from me as well. The rope stretch had simply absorbed all the energy, so it was like a parachute jump! Christine had difficulty there too, because she'd been waiting in the wind for the best part of half an hour for the two of us to do the pitch. The rest of that route was first rate. Lucky Tony Greenbank, discovering it as late as 1958. Did you climb it with Bill? I can thoroughly recommend it.

Anyway, Nigel insisted on leading the first pitch of Engineer's. This was so that I could get some reasonable pictures of him from the top of the ridge. We ended up with the doctor 120ft up

Christine Pearson moving across to the steep crack on Engineer's Slabs

Engineer's Slabs, Christine belayed at the bottom and me at the other end of her rope 150ft away on Sledgate Ridge. Talk about taking up the space! The two blokes who we'd overtaken must have thought us pretty silly.

The first pitch is brilliant, isn't it? Continuously steep and technical, it reminded me of Cairngorm classics. Just enough on that first few moves, of course; but I bet lots of people get put off by the first 15ft. Looking up, the whole face seems to be rearing up and toppling over on you, doesn't it?

I've told you about the sentry box, haven't I? The moves from crack to crack I thought were reasonable. There's that good flake, remember? And excellent handholds before the steep crack to the overhang level. I remember climbing most of that on the left wall. At the stance, I could inspect what must have been the remains of one of Balcombe's pegs. Even though it was not being used as part of the belay, it came as something of a shock to me when I touched it and the little bit of shaft that was left fell off! The good doctor had contrived a most complex multiple belay to which he had attached me many times; but I don't mind telling you in the privacy of this letter

Nigel Birtwell sorting out a runner after the lay-back on Engineer's Slabs

that, after that little incident I had a surreptitious check of each of the belay nuts in turn. I needn't have bothered, of course.

By the time Christine had arrived on the stance, we had been wrapped around again in a cold blanket of cloud. The doctor, it seemed, had, with Machiavellian cunning, engineered it so that it was impossible for us to unclip from any of the belays without upsetting the equilibrium of the human pyramid we had become. At least, that was what it may have looked like to anyone who could see and overhear us as I protested loudly about the job of the photographer, etc. In reality, the mechanical machinations were all mine so that I could guarantee Nigel would lead the horror-show pitch!

Well, to cut a long story short, I'm deeply and selfishly thankful that it was him up there and not me. For thirty minutes we were treated to the most alarming and unusual sight of the doctor (who's only 5ft 6in) bridged at his limit for move after move, doing impossible-looking stretches and actually sounding quite afraid. He put in eight runners and didn't appear to recover his equanimity until he'd had a few minutes to recover at the top. And he leads E2 with ease! Christine and I were almost numb with cold and fear. When it came my turn to follow, I put a brave face on it (for Christine's sake, you understand); but secretly wondered if Nigel would have the strength and stamina left to haul my not inconsiderable weight up the bomb bay chimney.

In the event, my expensive thermofleece jacket saved the day. Every desperate bridge for Nigel, I found I could reach with ease, being 6ft 2in. And my jacket, jammed uncompromisingly against the left wall of the groove, simply soaked up all the slime and muck that coated every dimple and hold within sight so that I could actually friction quite a bit. That's not to say I found it easy, of course. Those final moves are the worst. Do you remember the green slab with no holds on it you are supposed to bridge against, the absence of holds on the left wall and the perfect thread round the finishing block 5ft above your head? I think I simply crammed every appendage into every possible torquing point I could see and tried to press the rock apart. At the top, it came as a great surprise to both of us that I'd managed it without a tight rope; but I'm quite convinced that if I'd had to lead it, I would have needed some aid. Balcombe must have been a genius to climb it on sight without a runner.

When Christine had shivered up, we stood around in the cloud meekly, aware of the achievement, then and now. The doctor pronounced himself well pleased with all our efforts and very impressed. Glad, too, that he hadn't been manoeuvred out of the lead. I kept quiet about the machinations until it struck me that it was getting rather dark. Just as we were passing the summit cairn in thick cloud, I asked Nigel for the time. 'You'll never guesss,' he said, and then made me. David, can you believe it was half-past five on Sunday night? I had to be in school in Salisbury at eight the next morning for a meeting. So that's why we didn't call in on the way home – that, and the fact that all the North of England seemed to be either going to or coming from Blackpool Illuminations by motorway.

There's a postscript to this little adventure. It wasn't until break time at eleven the next day that I realised I'd been talking to the Head with half of Gable Crag still under my fingernails! Oh well, you win some and lose others; but I don't think she'd have understood about winning on Engineer's Slabs, do you?

See you soon, I hope.

Cheers, Tim.

Christine Pearson starting the final chimney of Engineer's Slabs in cloud

The Walk from Gable Crag to Burnthwaite

After Engineer's Slabs it is a simple matter to collect the sacks and return to the summit of Great Gable – perhaps the third time you will have visited it during the day – and descend directly southwest through the White Napes to Gavel Neese and the steep Moses Trod path (or reach the same spot by a more decorous western descent to the Beckhead path which joins the latter path at Moses' Finger). If you've got the energy left in the knees after 3–3¾ miles (5–6km) and a few thousand feet (approximately 610m) of ascent and descent, you can run down this steep path in 15 minutes to Burnthwaite. The Wasdale Head Hotel should be reached in a further 20 minutes.

9 E·S·K·D·A·L·E

The Walk from Hardknott Pass to Heron Crag

This is the longest day in the book – some 10 miles (16km) and several thousand feet (approximately 610m) of ascent and descent. Camp near Boot, get up very early and start to walk as the sun is rising. After parking at the foot of Hardknott Pass, follow the good track to Brotherilkeld. Cross the River Esk and then follow the good path on the northern bank all the way to Heron Crag. In track shoes and going well, you should be there in 40 minutes. Leave the sacks below the crag; you must descend to meet the path below the crag again.

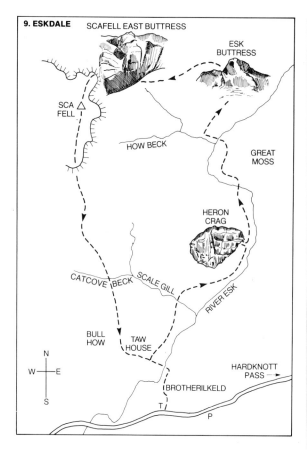

Upper Eskdale in a storm showing the route from Heron Crag (left centre) to Esk Buttress in the middle distance

MYTHICAL SIGNALS

Bellerophon (4b, 4c, 4c, 4c), Heron Crag (O. R. D. Pritchard and B. S. Schofield, May 1958)

After obtaining possession of the winged horse, Pegasus, Bellerophon rose with him into the air and slew the chimera with his arrows.

(*A Smaller Classical Dictionary*, Blakeney)

A mile (1.6km) or so up the Esk from Brotheril-keld, the river has scalloped hollows in the bedrock. On balmy days, midges dance impoten-tly over green sphagnum sponges and sheep stand in the deep bracken, stupefied by the heat. Some 300ft (91m) above on the hillside stands Heron Crag, its long, clean, slender central pillar – the magnet line of Gormenghast – drawn haughtily away from the churning pools. But as you scramble up the boulder field below the crag through hot vegetation and strong-smelling sheep scrapes, it is not the grey pillar which claims attention, but the deep-set groove that divides the crag into light and dark. This is the line of Pritchard and Schofield's climb of 1958, Bellerophon. It looks a horror – a real chimera. This is because the groove is water-worn and dead-bone white and its walls are strung with soft black purses of moss

that have burst and dribbled over every hold. But the guide-book tells us that although it is 'rather mossy, it can be climbed in wet conditions'.

Gearing up at the foot of a blunt and awkward-looking rib, I thought that might be taking the idea of adventure a little too far; and I remembered how, fifteen years ago in Norway, Renny Croft and I had shared precisely those sorts of adventures the last time we had climbed together.

As I set off up the 40ft (12m) of rib to a ledge and massive block belay, Renny's quiet ironic grin brought back memories of those long and often frightening nights in the sun when I had been forced to learn how to climb moss-filled cracks or, troll-like, sit down and turn to stone. From the ledge, three steps right take you straight onto the hairy holds of the groove. Renny led on through. It is obviously a vertical water-course, a crag drain; and here, when the rains come, a little bulge that has to be bridged and semi-mantled will produce a gurgling water-fall. The holds are positive but slight and I found the bridging tricky because I was cautious about smearing on the black medallions of lichen.

Renny grinned when I arrived puffing loudly. 'Somewhat heavier than when we climbed together in Norway,' he observed laconically and leaned back easily in his belay slings below a steep black crack. 'Do you remember when we did the South face of Skagastoltind in the Jotunheim, and you kept gibbering about the mossy cracks and how the atmosphere was intimidating? Well, look at this; it's your lead!' I tried to appear indifferent to his teasing. The problem for me then had really been one of clarity of perspective. Everywhere you go in Norway, images of the trolls, the gods and heroes are present in the place names and in the rock itself. Childhood stories of the frost giants dodging behind a mountain to avoid Thor's hammer, or of Peer Gynt, caught deep within the hill in the hall of the mountain king, seem quite plausible when you see the Jotunheim and the Dovrefjell. Mythical signals intruded into the climbing to such an extent that I found it almost impossible, then and subsequently, to separate the images of rock from the images of myths.

The author and Renny Croft on the first pitch of Bellerophon (Richard Brown)

Renny Croft leading the second pitch of Bellerophon (Richard Brown)

(right) John Baker struggling out of the slimy final crack of Bellerophon (Renny Croft)

The stories of gods and heroes eventually get overlaid by other stories of the lives of ordinary folk, of course. It's the same with climbs and climbers. What was once the hardest climb in the world becomes a warm-up for the best; he who was once a god in climbing terms grows old, gets killed or gives it up. But the point is this: the stories interlock on the rock. We re-create those myths when we speak of our own climbs.

The third pitch of Bellerophon looks immediately awkward and intimidating, a real arctic crack, for 40ft (12m) of corner with retaining walls draped in velvet lichen face the climber. These walls feel to the hand like the old-fashioned table cover in my Aunt Mary's dining-room: smooth and reassuring, but ultimately deceptive (she was my dentist); and I had to move from hidden foothold to hidden foothold, feeling with my feet under the lichen drapes for the holds. The corner offered cracked edges that could be gripped hard with impunity, but the walls contained only little knobbles from which bold bridges had to be built across the groove. I climbed it furiously, determined to deflect Renny's gentle irony with a show of style and determination. Towards the top, a huge bucket hold on the right wall lured me out of the crack, but like those lines of pegs that you are tempted to follow on big alpine classics, it was a dead end.

A slight struggle and final bridge landed me in a dark crypt-like niche. Another pull out left onto a pinnacle edge followed, and I could take a cramped belay on the ledge overlooking the corner. I leaned out from the eaves looking like a brightly coloured gargoyle and I called for Renny to follow. Then I stood in the drips from the black nose above and fell into the reverie that often overtakes me after a strenuous pitch. The regular, almost mesmeric movement of taking in the rope induced a feeling of contentment despite the damp and my tired fingers, and almost tempted me to make up a myth about myself and not about the climb. Luckily, however, I was rudely awakened from these preposterous Promethean day-dreams by the sudden, eagle-like arrival of my partner who was loudly complimentary about the pitch but not about the lead. In minutes he was off again, rising effortlessly around the sodden bulge and flying up the final overhanging crack. It was good he was leading. If the last pitch was 4c, this must surely be 5a – perhaps harder in the wet.

Renny slowed down on the final moves, looking for the sequence that would set him free of the corner. His workman-like approach to the pitch was a model for a myth-maker: he made those technical and strenuous jams look easy, as if he had known them all his life, and at the top, called down to say that it was a cinch and straight 4c. Reality again. I knew I would not find the pitch the same and, sure enough, for 80ft (24m) felt gross and clumsy, full of poisons. No hubris now – he's always been a better climber than me.

The finger jams felt very poor and slimy. A swing on the last runner was a great temptation, but Renny could see my every move. With the last vestiges of style and strength I found the holds to move out left and crawled up the final slab to the belay. What a route. So easy in that final crack to fall if you get the sequence wrong. Just like poor Bellerophon at the end of his story.

After coiling the rope, I lay down on the rock in a watery sun. The weather was breaking quickly. Heavy grey clouds were boiling over Hardknott Pass, scouring the hills clean. I thought of the long walk ahead to Esk Buttress and then Scafell and yearned for a horse or wings. 'What are you dreaming about now, then?' Renny asked incuriously, as he threw me my gear.

'I'm dreaming of Pegasus,' I replied, trying as hard as possible to be ironic inside the mythical frame. 'We're going to need him getting to Medusa Wall.'

Pitch four of Bellerophon: John Baker climbs the overhang, watched carefully by Richard Brown (Renny Croft)

The Walk from Heron Crag to Esk Buttress

From Heron, follow the true right bank of the Esk to the bend and marshes at Scar Lathing. This is perhaps one of the most beautiful sections of path in Lakeland with views down into scores of delectable pools in the Esk river. Cross the river at Scar Lathing (in track shoes, it doesn't matter if you get wet, because it's ten to one the Great Moss will be damp anyway, but pack some dry socks!).

The path turns north into the startling upper Esk Valley. So like a Himalyan valley leading to a pass (in this case, Esk Hause, away to the north), this wide open space prepares you for the bulk of Cam Spout Crag on the left and eventually, Esk Buttress. Another crossing of the Esk will be necessary, though, before you can scramble to its base. It is highly desirable to carry sacks on Medusa Wall (as the essay makes quite clear). A grassy ramp leads over a col from the summit of the crag, almost on the contour lines to Mickledore. Certainly, from the top of Medusa Wall to the bottom of Mickledore Grooves, it is a matter of less than an hour. But you may have to trade energy against speed by carrying the sacks up that crux wall.

STONEWALLING

Medusa Wall (4c, 4a, 4c, 4b), Esk Buttress (A. R. Dolphin and L. J. Griffin, August 1947)

'Mirror, mirror, on the wall, who is the [strongest] of them all?'

(Traditional)

We broke no records getting to Esk Buttress: even with wind assistance, our times were nearly half an hour over guide-book standard. Gossip, photo-poses, drinks and rests accounted for the deficit; but friendships notwithstanding, it was obvious that covertly we were really sprinting for the cliff. There was no official competition, you understand – no one had actually declared a race. It was just that as we picked our own routes over sunken grey stone walls across the vast forgotten garden of Great Moss, each pair of climbers endeavoured to keep in touch, vying for the lead as if on rock, trying to beat the other pair to the prize of the climb. Ian and I got to the crag-foot last. He had stopped to take two panoramas with his new Nikon; I was just tired. It was a month over twenty-six years since that famous race between Pete Crew's and Allan Austin's teams for the Central Pillar had occurred; but we, I hoped, had designs on a harmonious ascent of a much easier route: Arthur Dolphin's Medusa Wall.

While Ian and I changed frantically, David Craig sorted through his antique collection of hexes and Terry Gifford pulled on a pair of yellow designer trousers. Renny Croft, already harnessed and gazing thoughtfully at the heavy cumulus through clouds of cigar smoke, was humming Bach. It was nearly midday.

Esk Buttress is a Gothic cathedral of a crag. Above a 100ft (30m) broken crypt of rock and vegetation, massive stone curtains, hung from flying buttresses of fell, lean in towards a central mass of clean grey pillars, grooved and finely wrought. As we swung in slings like wind-vanes below Square Chimney, we could see clearly above us the filigree chalk-finger work on the cliff's finest creation, The Cumbrian. This was the day's aim for our reserve team, the 'Bath Vegetarian Bike Boys', supported by 'Mickey, The Amazing Climbing Dog'.

Medusa Wall is something of a hybrid climb, sharing pitches with Square Chimney and Bridge's Route; but it is as direct, clean and sustained as any other VS in Lakeland. The Constable guide warns that on the chimney pitch: 'Medium-sized climbers will be able to adopt a back-and-foot position (just) but shorter men will have to bridge (much harder).' This is somewhat hard on shorter women, perhaps, but accurate. Renny, who is 5ft 8in (1.75m) pulled his flat cap over his eyes and set off bridging like an Olympian. Ian, super-glued to his Nikon, almost fell over himself and his belay with excitement, trying to get the definitive shot of Renny's elegant pirouettes; but when the rope came tight for him to climb, he found it hard to chimney against his huge camera bag.

I shuffle up in Sally's new cagoule, not frictioning well on the left wall with my back, but finding toesticks all right. My apprehension as I climb has less to do with the rock than with my wife: I cannot face her if I've grazed the Gore-Tex of her week-old birthday present. Eventually, of course, I have to swing into a bridge and, as I rest on good edges, glimpse Mickey doing outrageous standing somersaults 100ft (30m) below.

It is best to continue straight up the steep crack on the right. Jim Birkett's Square Chimney traverses left over a repulsive mossy slab into a steep corner, but after any rain, it weeps for ages and looks unlikely on the best of days.

'Press on,' said Renny, soaking up the sun. 'David and Terry are already on the last moves.' So I run pitches five and six of Bridge's Route into one and creep tensely up the slick and greasy gully to a bulge. With over 120ft (36m) of rope run out on a dog-leg through four runners, I am beginning to double my weight on the holds. Hauling wet slack and holding it momentarily in my teeth, I can place and clip a Friend under the overlap, quickly, and bridge the gully walls before I'm stopped with a jerk by the rope. A perfect thread at the back of the gully provides the belay and a stunning view of the final pitch – the cracked wall and arête.

It is sheltered at this stance and I can take off my cagoule and sweater. Soon, Ian arrives below the little overhang. 'I wonder if you can keep the rope tight, here, Tim,' he says. 'I think I've hurt me back.' He burrows away at the bulge, mole-busy and purposive. 'Oooh, me back!' he snorts loudly, pulling powerfully onto the ledge.

Esk Buttress, 'a Gothic cathedral of a crag' (Ian Smith)

'Bridging like an Olympian', Renny Croft makes progress up the Square Chimney on Medusa Wall

'Ian,' I tell him, 'it's not your back that's hurting, it's the Nikon pouch with the fifteen lenses that's giving you the pain. Can't you feel the hunch-pack pressure on your back!'

'Ah, yes,' he says, 'perhaps it is. Now, will you watch the ropes while I go up there and find the best camera-angle?'

I watch him carefully as he pads up through the grass and digs himself a settee-stance. I give him lots of rope and he belays around a foxglove clump. Renny is with us in minutes. We retie for me to lead the wall.

This is an ambition. A Chris Bonington black and white photograph of Richard McHardy and Martin Boysen, printed in *Rocksport* years ago, and now again in *Cumbrian Rock* has been an inspiration to climb this pitch. But I find I can't.

I get one of Dick Turnbull's special nuts well seated half-way up the crack, then fail to find the sequence on the wall and get the nut out. Renny is not amused. It is while I'm trying to find the strength to finish that I recall the guide-books: 'Take the *central* of three grooves above to the top of the pinnacle, then move right . . .' But the photo of McHardy shows him in the *outside* 'groove'! Which is right? This outside crack-cum-groove certainly feels VS and is much harder-looking than the central groove. The guide-books must be wrong. If they're not, they ought to be: this is the crack to sort the strong from the weak.

Defensive, pumped, peeved after four attempts and four repetitions, variously stressed of 'I'm going to do it now', I plead with Renny to do it, which he does: climbing somehow not in the crack and wall but on his shadows in the mirror-stone, half-turned away, sun-struck, looking like Perseus must have done, not at Medusa but into the polished shield of self.

When Ian has gone as well, and the single 9mm from him to me has been unclipped from all the runners, I need to stand on the ledge and look down on Central Pillar and The Cumbrian to get the crack into perspective. Derek 'Digits'

Toulalan, John and Dave are strung out on Central Pillar, quite relaxed. No dogging needed today apparently, because they're well within their grade. 'A bit too cold to try 6b,' DDT calls contentedly up at me, while 200ft (61m) below, Mickey barks excitedly as he sees us, and tries a first terrier ascent of one of the big boulders below the crag.

The crack is technical and awkward, strenuous and steep. I have to make long stretches to reach each flat hold and edge. Renny has bypassed the stance on the pillar-edge, so this pitch is now 100ft (30m) of exposed 4c/4b. The tendons in my right arm feel strained; I need to stop and breathe before the final delicate rib which is wildly exposed. This is best climbed quickly and direct. On the terrace, the wind tugs insistently at us all. David and Terry have already left for the East Buttress of Scafell – in running shoes and rock boots. But fortunately, Ian has run out of film. We will have to go back down 600ft (183m) to the sacks before we can follow them to Mickledore.

It is 5 o'clock by the time we have packed the sacks and had a bite to eat. 'Do you really want to go up to Scafell now and finish off the day properly?', Renny asks me. Ian is either diplomatically quiet or genuinely busy with his camera. I prevaricate, am non-committal, stone wall once again. Half of the 'Bath Bike Team' have already cycled home in search of vegetarian food; the other half, still on the Pillar, scream down their disbelief when at last, more out of shame than strength of will, I commit the four of us to another climb.

As we set off up the hill, Mickey bounces round us, as fresh and as strong as when he started his day, obviously eager to scamper to the top of England. It made me think. Perseus, had he been offered the mythical prize of a strong climbing dog instead of a flying horse after cutting Medusa down to size, would surely have opted for the dog.

The Walk from Esk Buttress to Scafell East Buttress

At the summit of Esk Buttress, the hillside intrudes gently. A grassy ramp-line, following gentle contours rises almost due west to the Cam Spout path and Mickledore. Scafell East Buttress is just over a kilometre from Esk Buttress, but if you take the wrong line to the Cam Spout path, you can spend a lot of time scrambling over strength-sapping screes. If in doubt, keep high, with Mickledore in sight. The climb starts below a bulge and an obvious rightwards sloping gangway a few metres down from Mickledore Chimney.

Renny Croft tackles the crux of Medusa Wall, the cracked wall (Ian Smith)

IN THE MEDALS AGAIN

Mickledore Grooves (4c, 4c), Scafell East Buttress (C. F. Kirkus, I. M. Waller and M. Pallis, May 1951)

For when the One Great Scorer comes
To write against your name,
He marks – not that you won or lost –
But how you played the game.

('Alumnus Football', Grantland Rice)

From the Cam Spout path, Scafell East Buttress looks like an old stone wall on a fellside, mole-weakened and bulging dangerously. But close up, at the toe of the buttress – the line of Lost Horizons – its true nature is revealed. This is Falstaff's heaven, a split cask of a cliff, spigotted at random, squirting and dribbling from a hundred places. Barrel walls are split down the seams, oozing black caulking. High angle bands of slabs, sprung, discontinuous and hanging in space, cling to its massive girth. Touch the cliff too hard and it will surely burst asunder, spilling the mountain.

Under the dank side, close to Mickledore, a series of steeply inclined ramps morticed into overhanging cracks and grooves lead out of the impending walls. It is an intimidating place at the best of times, early in the morning. But if you stand here in the evening, deep in the lees of shadow, after tons of rain have seeped down through the press of stone and contemplate a climb, you need to be inspired.

In 1931, Colin Kirkus with Marco Pallis and Ivan Waller found the entry to the big hanging slab close to Broad Stand that had eluded H. M. Kelly some years before. Kelly had tried the logical entry – the slabs out of Mickledore Chimney (now the line of Barry's Traverse and the start of the East Buttress Girdle); but Kirkus took the overhang and rightwards-slanting grooves, the line of most resistance, to get established on the slab. The pitch that followed, out across the slab, over the overlap, into and up the bottomless groove, was a masterpiece of technical ability and courage. Kirkus at a stroke showed what was possible on this facet of the

Renny Croft approaching the wet bit on the first pitch of Mickledore Grooves

cliff. And he did it in the finest style, leading what was then the longest hard pitch in the Lakes – 140ft (43m) – without a runner, in three-quarters of an hour. Marco Pallis's photograph of Waller seconding the pitch shows just what a feat it was: the groove has spewed great gouts of lichen down the slab and Waller, his white gym shoes highlighted against the black deposits, is toe-balancing precariously across the upper slab. Kirkus hasn't cheated on the route: the lichen is unbrushed, the slab uncleaned. Perhaps that is why he had so many falls in his career: climbing from the ground; going for the prizes honestly.

Mickledore Grooves is both strenuous and delicate. The technical crux is getting off the ground, but the long and (even now) poorly protected groove above the slab is the mental crux. It is much harder when it is wet.

Standing in the evening wind below the overhanging crack of Dyad while Renny forced the first groove, I thought it was raining. But according to Ian, who was looking through a long lens, it was just the slabs of Mayday emptying their slops 50ft (15m) above me.

'Leave the orange sling on that little bollard, please, Renny,' I had asked him after he had bridged and hauled over the crux bulge. Fifteen years ago with Ian Jackson, lighter and less afraid, I had led this crux without a thought before going on to Mayday; but now some aid might be needed. Ivan Waller, quoted in *Cumbrian Rock*, admits that time changes one's attributes and ethics when he recalls that: 'Each pitch has a strenuous fingery move which I thoroughly enjoyed, but when I was taken up it 43 years later, I needed aid for both of them.' At sixty odd, though, that isn't too much to worry about!

At 15ft (4.5m) up a groove, Renny exclaimed about the wet and swung round into the right-hand branch. In no time he was calling for me to follow.

The moves out of the top of this constricted righthand groove are steep and thin on rock that is marblesmooth. The footholds for the left foot are little more than scored lines; for the right, slick bridges underneath a bulge. With hands wrapped tightly over a rounded edge, you try to ease yourself out of the bottleneck, corkscrew torquing to get maximum leverage on the contact points. The sloping ledge and big flake belay come just in time.

Renny Croft and the author starting Mickledore Grooves (Ian Smith)

It was from this ledge that Menlove Edwards saved Wilfred Noyce's life. Noyce had already failed to climb the crux without some aid from Menlove and was nervous. He called out that he would need a lot of beer that night. Then, as he turned the step at the top of the wet groove, in socks, without a runner behind him, he stepped onto a sod of turf already loosened by the rain. John Wilkinson in *Mountain 30* gives an account of what happened next – an account which is rounded out by Jim Perrin in *Menlove*:

> *As Noyce fell down the groove, Edwards took in some slack, and with the rope running behind the grass ledge, took the strain. The 170ft rope . . . stretched, and, as two strands parted, Noyce touched down on the ground. He was fortunate to survive a fall of 200 feet with only a few broken bones in face and hand.*

Noyce and Edwards were staying with Professor Pigou at Lower Gatesgarth in Buttermere. It was his habit, apparently, to award medals for 'notable feats of incompetence'. After a long convalescence at Gatesgarth, Noyce received a leather medal for his Mickledore Grooves performance.

It is quite impossible now, as you step up onto the delicate slab and balance towards the diagonal crack that cuts down through the overlap above, to do the same as Noyce. Four wire runners in 40ft (12m) protect the slab, should that be what you need; but the move over the overlap with fingers in a muddy pocket is still a stopper if you lack the bottle. As with most slabs, especially in the wet, the best technique is not to stop. There is an awkward rest at the foot of the groove to head for and the rusty marks of two old pegs that some cheat put in quite soon after Kirkus's first ascent. Protection in the smooth groove is not immediately apparent and a leader has to feel very confident about bridging on friction.

At my request, Renny had gone on leading before the light failed. Ian was still sitting Buddha-like below the col, staring into the

Renny Croft and the author embark upon the slabby second pitch of Mickledore Grooves (Ian Smith)

viewfinder at us, practising the Zen of photography, summoning up the light. Calling the shots, he asked Renny to doff the green flat cap so that what sky light was left would shine on his receding golden hair. By the time I was in the groove, though, it was almost dark.

Round an awkward edge, 120ft (36m) from the stance, the stone foundation of that fateful grassy sod is crept over soberly. A final tricky wall is all that is left to climb.

I had had no falls, but two tight ropes on pitch one and one submission in the lead. This counts as failure in Renny's rule book which states that you must give the rock a chance. And I think he's right. If you need a pull, you couldn't lead cleanly. There are, or should be, no medals for cheating, competing with the rock. Possessing far more sophisticated means of protecting our leads than did our forebears, surely we should be aiming to emulate the style of those pure first ascents; aiming to improve the boldness of our climbing, rather than the skill with which we fix a runner?

But I knew that the Bath teams would be delighted with the news of my struggles and would claim a drink from me in the Burnmoor for every moment of the day I had leaned illegally on rope. So, as we hurried down Broad Stand in a short, sharp shock of hail, under a deep black hangover of cloud, I tried to work out how much beer a barrel really holds and how I could stay out of the medals in future.

The Walk from Scafell East Buttress to Brotherilkeld

Mickledore Grooves will be taxing late in the day, but get the second to carry the sacks, one stuffed inside the other. If you don't, you will have to descend Broad Stand and then either reascend it to the summit or retreat via the Cam Spout path. A sublime finish to the day, though, is to grit the teeth and scramble over broken rock some 220yd (200m) south and west to the summit of Scafell. With luck, the sun will be dipping and the views to every point of the compass will be unbeatable. The way back home is obvious: down the broad, well-worn southerly path to Horn Crag and lower Eskdale. At Cat Crag, just after the path has passed the superb defile of Catcove Beck, take a short-cut directly down the hill beside Scale Gill. The path from Brotherilkeld is joined in minutes.

10 C·O·N·I·S·T·O·N

The Walk from Walna Scar road to Dow Crag

It may seem perverse to start a day's climbing on Dow Crag by walking away from the crag, but the leg stretch, the view, the whole context of the climbing is established by the view from The Old Man. It is sensible to park just after the gate on the Walna Scar road and then follow the prepared path up through the quarries to the summit. This is straightforward, if strenuous (but if you have followed us round, you will at least be fit). A contour round to meet the climber's path which leads back underneath the buttresses of Dow Crag is also a formality, as indeed is the descent to the shores of Goat's Water and return to the cars by the well-worn Walna Scar road. But it is a magnificent mountain day.

TIGER, TIGER

Murray's Direct (4c, 4b, 4c), B Buttress, Dow Crag (Tiger Traverse, September 1921; The Link Pitch, August 1945; The Direct Finish, October 1922: various parties)

'Only a Tiger could get up that.'

(George Bower to Harry Griffin)

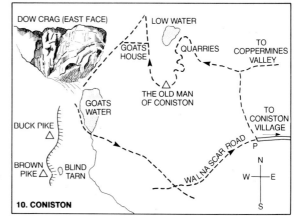

10. CONISTON

In the 1920s there were four main groups of climbers operating in the Lakes. Based, not surprisingly because of the difficulties of transport, on the main towns round the perimeter of the district – Kendal, Keswick, Penrith and Barrow – they tended to monopolise the crags which were nearest to their base. In general, these bases remain much the same today, although Ambleside is now a centre in its own right, and, because of better transport, the teams tend now to come out of the south and north of Cumbria than out of individual towns (see Trevor Jones's *Cumbrian Rock* for a full account of the regional rivalry within the Lake District down the years). But the western fells and crags have always had their aficionados. Ennerdale and Wasdale are immediately accessible from the coast; Coniston is almost closer to the sea than it is to Windermere. And after World War I, according to Trevor Jones, the increase in leisure hours, the proliferation of the motor car and, above all, the important Vickers Engineering works at Barrow-in-Furness, combined to produce a sudden upsurge in climbing standards throughout the Lake District. This was very much the case on Dow Crag.

The small band of dedicated climbers based in Barrow in those early post-war years contained some of the greatest names of the sport as a whole. George Bower, H. S. Gross, George Basterfield and J. I. Roper – perhaps the leading lights of their generation – pushed forward the standards and opened up the cliffs. Roper's Black Wall and Great Central Route, both on Dow, are still graded HVS. The crux of the latter at 5b is quite as hard as Herford and Sansom's famous prewar breakthrough at the same grade on Central Buttress, Scafell. George Bower is credited with the 'discovery' of Esk Buttress and of course climbed the classic Hard Severe on that cliff which bears his name.

It was into this burgeoning scene that the

young Harry Griffin stepped – quite literally, in fact, because he asked to see the climbing mayor of Barrow, George Basterfield, in person. The full tale of Harry's teenage presumption, calling on the mayor in his parlour to enquire whereabouts the best nailed boots were to be bought, is told in full in Harry's inimitable way in *Long Days in the Hills* and *In Mountain Lakeland*. But George Basterfield was obviously impressed by the young Griffin's boldness, for it was he who introduced Harry Griffin to a lifetime's climbing by taking him on his first day on rock, 'up Woodhouse's Route, down Easter Gully, up Arête, Chimney and Crack and down Great Gully'. On Woodhouse's, Harry's first route, they climbed the direct start and George insisted that Harry lead the final pitch. If there could be any better advertisement for the patience, skill and judgement of a master climber and teacher than the following expression of heart-felt thanks from Harry, I have not heard it. It reminds me, as a teacher who has taught young people 'how to climb', that the teaching (and the learning) is a long and arduous moral process, rooted in respect for persons, rocks and the forms of social interaction long associated with the sport. These are, indubit-ably, the 'things . . . that matter'.

To George, who kept me under his wing for some time, I owe the joy that followed of many hundreds of days on the crags, the discovery of scores of things about rocks and mountains that matter, and the company of a host of interesting people who accepted a rather naive adolescent because I was a friend of George.

Living in Barrow, Harry used to catch the workmen's train from there to Torver, early in the morning, and then walk up the Walna Scar road to the cliffs. While walking, he learned all sorts of odd things to do with cragging, such as the fact that Sansom recommended barley sugar to make the fingers sticky for hard climbing, but that George (Basterfield) inclined to grapefruit juice. (Apparently oranges were deemed unsuitable because they don't get sticky enough.) Grapefruit after World War I must have been at least five times as expensive as modern chalk, and one wonders where they could be obtained and how much juice was needed to provide sufficient 'stick'!

But it was not simply helpful hints young Harry learned. On one occasion, walking with George up to Dow, Harry noticed some boot marks in the mud. 'Ah, yes,' George observed on looking closely at them, 'that must be Billy Clegg and A. T. Hargreaves; I know the patterns of their nails.' Apparently, everyone used Stephens of Coniston to nail their boots, but the patterns were bespoke.

George's careful teaching paid off because in 1931, Griffin was third man on the first ascent of a tricky little 4c pitch that led into the bottom of the long corner which dominates the classic Severe of B Buttress, Murray's Climb.

Although short, it was not insignificant in the scheme of things, because it led to the creation of the hybrid climb of Murray's Direct, one of the finest short VS climbs in England. Each pitch of this route had been climbed separately with years elapsing before the climb was completed in 1945. Each pitch has something good to offer the keen collector of routes; indeed, it is a perfect place to teach and learn the demanding basic techniques of climbing at this grade: balance, friction, finger-locks, lay-backs, fist and finger jams. But if the rock is wet at all (and in bad weather a lurid satin sheen graces much of the lay-back and the delicate slab of the traverse pitch), it can become a real test piece.

Richard Brown and I climbed it in a hot spell in 1987 when the friction was superb and the green lichen at the top of the lay-back was no more than an ancient stain. It was Richard's first VS climb. We had climbed a lot together in Scotland on snow and ice, but rock in the sun requires a different technique. Every move for Richard had to be learned the hard and painful way: initially, he couldn't understand how he was supposed to use the single finger holds to pull onto the faceted slab. And then he couldn't, wouldn't, trust the friction of his soles against the rock to move across towards the slanting slab. Beyond that, though, he learned how to manage fast – as you would expect, since he is the headmaster of a primary school – and, being strong in the upper body from hours of badminton, he pulverised the lay-back.

A telephoto shot of Dow Crag from the summit of Coniston Old Man. A buttress is the sunlit one to the left of Great Gully; Murray's Direct rises from the stretcher box at the foot of the next buttress, B and follows the steep corner above

Starting the lay-back crack of Murray's Direct

The author and Richard Brown completing Tiger Traverse on Murray's Direct (John Baker)

But on a later venture, a day's outing from Sheffield with Ian Smith, Bill Dark and Steve Walker, the traverse gleamed evilly in a dangerous light. Other teams were earnestly attempting and retreating from Murray's slab around the corner as Bill muscled up onto the crux of Tiger Traverse. Working for a national building inspection firm in between long bouts of Antarctic Survey work makes him somewhat scornful of 'conditions': a little water wasn't going to prevent him from doing the deed.

However, the lay-back was very hard in those conditions. I know, because I swung and looked at it for an hour and a half in a winter wind while Steve and the Sheffield Tigers sorted out the moves. The crack is wide with a positive, if bulky, edge; and the wall is steeper than it looks. The final delicacies up the crack in the wall to the right remind one of the moves away from the Hammer lay-back on Etive Slabs: open and vulnerable after the fierceness of the crack. But

as you find the superb little sequence that takes you over the final bulge, 200ft (61m) above the scree, at least you will have the satisfaction of having learned to climb in style (and probably within an hour) a route, that started from the top down in the boom years of the 1920s, took another twenty-five to complete.

When George Bower told Harry Griffin that only a Tiger would get up that first pitch, Harry thought he meant a real tiger, of the striped, voracious kind. He hadn't learned the climbing jargon. In modern terms, the little traverse 'goes' easily enough to quite ordinary climbers; so when the sun shines, go up to B Buttress, put your lycra tiger tights on, spring at that first hold and then explore the 'fearful symmetry' of the wall and crack above. George Basterfield, if he had still been alive and watching from below, would not be able to believe his eyes. And he would probably wonder where you had got the fifteen grapefruits from!

THE SHOALS OF HEAVEN

Eliminate A (4b, 4b, 4c, 4b, 4c, 4b), A Buttress, Dow Crag (H. S. Gross and G. Basterfield, June 1923)

All knowledge is interpretation.

(Suzanne Langer)

If you can rise early enough, just after dark dawn, and climb quickly up the quarries path in shadow to the summit of Coniston Old Man, the sun will rise on you. Then, look into the far south and west: the sea will be blinding; in the north and west, the hills will be alight. The compact mass of Dow Crag will be warming, turning light grey on the spit of earth-spin under the sun, and the line of Eliminate A on A Buttress will be sharp and clear.

Hundreds of years before these cliffs were ever noticed by human beings, a huge rockfall must have occurred on A Buttress. It has left a distinctive and complicated recess, seamed with overhangs, some 200ft (61m) high. Eliminate A weaves a masterly line through this area, linking big features by cunning traverses in pitch after

pitch of the finest VS climbing to be found anywhere in Britain, eliminating extreme difficulty either by wandering sublimely around it or ignoring it. Not surprisingly, the Constable guide gives the climb three stars and calls it 'magnificent'. The route was the last of the eliminates to be climbed, but it is the best and, like B and C before it, was the product of that brilliant, if ill-fated, climber, Bert Gross. The faithful Basterfield seconded him on each of these classics of the inter-war years, a fitting climax to the career of that large-spirited devotee of Dow.

The route starts on the very edge of A Buttress, overlooking the tortured rocks of Great Gully. Below the stance, a vast scree fan falls steeply to the shores of Goat's Water and then on down, into the deeps. Millions of tons of rubble, ice-levered from the buttress and frost shattered out of the gullies, provide a slowly moving platform below the steady plinth of cliff. This scree chute is surely a vision of a mountaineer's hell, especially if you try to reach the climb direct from the tarn. Here is the very place to wish your enemies; here they could try and outdo Sisyphus by rolling all that stone back up the hill to

Bill Dark pulls boldly onto a very wet Tiger Traverse, Dow Crag (Ian Smith)

David Craig high on Eliminate A having combined the
first two pitches (John Baker)

'The shoals of Heaven': Dow Crag from the shores of
Goat's Water

reconstruct the missing front of A Buttress, piece by piece. Eternity would not be long enough. But above the plinth, a steep clean rib is scored by a spiral weakness which leads further up a wall to where the cliff lifts it black visor to show nothing but frowning overhangs.

Richard was apprehensive as I explored carefully, up and round the steep helter-skelter groove of stone on the first pitch. He had done nothing like this climb. 'I know you've done it before,' he had said quietly, as we roped up in bright sunlight, 'so you know what to expect. But I'm afraid I won't be able to cope with those overhangs.' I explained to him then that the route moves left directly underneath the roof and swings up a weakness into a gully away on the opposite side to where we started. But he was unconvinced, I think, preferring for the moment at least his own interpretation of those uncompromising roofs. The signs of overhangs were signifying difficulty and fear.

I found the little spike that wobbled (just as I did when I reached for it) and moved up, on the edge, into a wider groove, and then, at 50ft (15m) onto the terrace. I knew from past ascents that I could reach the *rochers perchés* stance in one run out if I was careful how I placed the runners for my double ropes; so, placing two good ones in the back wall, I moved cautiously up into a slight scoop. I knew that this was not hard (there are good pressure holds, superb friction and small cracks), but it felt tricky. The mantelshelf came quickly and then, immediately, the ledge at the foot of the steep groove.

The climb starts to change here. Below this point it has been predominantly balance and friction; but above, the rock is more clean cut, steep and blocky. Some strength is needed now as well as good technique to bridge the groove and pull out left below the niche of the Raven's Nest. The first of the climb's three cruxes is 5ft (1.5m) away. Earlier on the same day, I had watched David Craig hesitate and wonder which way to go at this point. He had found the right-hand variant easier than going straight up the steep V-groove to the stance, and with his ancient single rope clipped into a short runner back in the groove below the Raven's Nest, was struggling to maintain his equanimity and balance against massive rope drag. Either way is technically exacting enough, especially with a lot of rope out. The broad but sloping belay ledge,

jutting out in space like a bow without a figurehead, is very welcome. I was sweating profusely when I reached it and sat down to rest in the small shadow of the overhang, feeling that I was in the front seat of the stalls. The sun was a brass trumpet blast. I could see Richard below me, a coloured dot on the grey screen of scree. Looking cautiously over the edge, I stared down at a harassed leader on the second pitch of Sidewalk, bleeding from bad knuckle grazes and pleading for a rope. I tried to pull some slack through quickly, forgetting in the hurry that I had led out the full rope length. But by the time I had realised why it wasn't pulling through, he had slumped down onto a runner and lowered off, cursing.

There are now no perched blocks in the little niche at the end of the belay ledge. A stunning black and white photograph by Chris Bonington of this crux pitch (reprinted in the FRCC Centenary Journal) shows a leader using these blocks and a high handhold to get onto the tiny ledge to the left. In fact, this move is simply not necessary, for, without the blocks, the grade is still the same. Here is a crux that can be done in a number of ways. After clipping the rusty peg 3ft (1m) from the belay (and then dismissing the illusory protection offered by that wafer-thin eye), it is possible to step out over the void onto small wall holds and reach across to the ledge with your hands. The higher version is to step into the niche with the right foot (thinking of the extra inches the absent blocks once gave to help the balance tilt towards the ledge), then to reach wide with the left and slap the bulging bulwark and pull through a weightless moment into loud insistent gravity again. Everything sticks and stays if the crux is dry. But, after a week of rain, this ledge is a Site of Special Scientific Interest where a hanging garden of mosses grows, dripping greenly.

It is tempting to scurry round the big white bulging slab that follows immediately (which is visible from miles away) into the angle underneath the roof to belay. Far better, though, to place a runner on a long sling and start the awkward crack which leads up to a bulge on the edge of all things. It is a miniature Murray's

David Craig engrossed in the difficult moves of Eliminate A on A Buttress, Dow Crag

Climb, traversing in a most exposed position but with huge handholds. At the end it gets somewhat harder as the pulpit stems below get thinner and the corrugations disappear. But runners are aplenty and once over the bulge, (re)union with the belay is only a moment away.

Richard was animated as we swapped gear, so much more confident after completing the lower pitches. I think it helped that for much of the time I couldn't see him and he was alone with the rock. Not once had he called for tight or slowed down. I read to him from the guide-book: 'Pitch 5. 50 feet (4c). A low traverse line across the very exposed slab on the right leads, boldly, into a groove which is followed directly to the Gordon and Craig's Traverse.'

'Is it really out there?' he asked me.

'Yes, I'm afraid it is,' I replied, none too sure that this was the pitch that I really wanted to do (see guide for variations here). But the FRRC 1987 guide has a picture of Karen Long crossing the hanging slab and it is unmistakable. Even if I hadn't seen that photo, John Cleare has another brilliant picture of Ian Howell on this pitch in *The World Guide to Mountains and Mountaineering* which would be an inspiration to any VS leader. Howell has stepped into space without a runner. The white quartz patches on B Buttress gleam eerily in the light reflected from the slopes of The Old Man opposite. The cliff falls away immediately below his feet.

I stepped onto nicks and held onto nicks, fingers dusted carefully against the heat. I relaxed mantra-like and balanced quickly across the ribs to a rest below the groove. Here, I could lean out and look up. A daring aeroplane had torn the big blue bag of the sky apart. There was another white sky bag inside the blue. My head was clear but it felt as if the cliff was moving. I held on tightly, an 'extravagant and wheeling stranger' in that vertical plane, feeling the axial spin of stone, sensing the radial sweep of air. The next few pulls, though terrifically exposed, led without difficulty to the Gordon and Craig Traverse. And then all that was left was just under 100ft (30m) of a steep, well-proportioned, liberally endowed crack at steady 4b.

We hurried down Easy Gully, ignoring the guidebook's warning about loose rock and finding a reasonably sound path down the gully wall. Richard's wife and children were basking by the water and we wanted to join them for some lunch while the sun was high.

From the shores of Goat's Water the full grandeur of the cliff is apparent; and the tarn mirrors the cliff. As I lazed out of time on a bank of cropped turf and watched the ripples move towards the pebbled shore, I remembered how, years ago, I had once misheard the title of a famous Ewan McColl song and gone around thinking that the 'Shoals of Herring' was actually the 'Shoals of Heaven'. Here, where some of the loveliest stones in Lakeland grow out of the tarn outfall, it is not difficult to let words go and set meanings to drift like the ripples across the water.

As shadows filled like pools of ink, we played on the stepping-stones for an hour, jumping backwards and forwards, not thinking of the life to come. We lay down and looked across the tarn at water level: the stones became islands in the stream; Dow Crag, the mountains of the moon.

Later, as the sun tucked over the hill and the children grew drowsy, we walked quietly back to Coniston. But all the way down the Walna Scar road I was still aground beside the water, on the shore, hearing the rhythmic tide of ripples, looking upside down at Dow Crag reared against the sky, hunting once again for the shoals of heaven.

B·I·B·L·I·O·G·R·A·P·H·Y

Bailey, Adrian, *Lakeland Rock* (W.P., 1985)

Birkett, Bill, *Lakeland's Greatest Pioneers* (Hale, 1983)

Cleare, John, *The World Guide to Mountains* (Webb & Bower, 1979)

Craig, David, *Against Looting* (Giant Steps, 1987)

— —, *Native Stones* (Secker & Warburg, 1988)

Cram, Eilbeck & Roper, *Rock Climbing in the Lake District* (Constable, 1975); (new ed) Cram, Eilbeck, Roper & Birkett (Constable, 1987)

Crew, Soper & Wilson, *The Black Cliff* (Kaye Ward, 1971)

FRCC Centenary Journal (1986)

FRCC Climbing Guides to: Great Langdale, Buttermere & Eastern Crags, Borrowdale, Pillar Rock, Great Gable, Scafell, Dow and Eskdale

FRCC Journal, Vol XII, No 2; Vol XIII, No 36; Vol XV, No 43

Gambles, R., *Lake District Place Names* (Dalesman, 1980)

General Recommendations from the 1984 Brockhole Conference on Adventure and Environmental Awareness

Gifford, Terry, *The Stone Spiral* (Giant Steps, 1987)

Griffin, Harry, *Long Days in the Hills* (Robert Hale, 1974)

— —, *In Mountain Lakeland* (Guardian Press, 1963)

Hankinson, Alan, *The First Tigers* (J. M. Dent & Sons, 1972)

Jones, Trevor, *Cumbrian Rock* (Pic, 1988)

Nicholson, Norman, *The Lake District: An Anthology* (Penguin, 1978)

Oppenheimer, Lehmann J., *The Heart of Lakeland* (The Ernest Press, 1988)

Peascod, Bill, *Journey After Dawn* (Cicerone Press, 1985)

Perrin, Jim, *Menlove* (Gollancz, 1985)

— — (ed) *Mirrors in the Cliffs* (Diadem, 1983)

Wilson, Ken, *Hard Rock* (Hart Davis McGibbon, 1975)

A·C·K·N·O·W·L·E·D·G·E·M·E·N·T·S

A book of this kind is rarely the product of the author's efforts alone, and this is no exception. I have been fortunate to share the days on these climbs with many friends who have given unstintingly of their time and skill. All better climbers than me, they have been forbearing and encouraging by turns; so thanks to friends Pete Clarke, Renny Croft, John Baker, Nigel Birtwell, Richard Brown, Bill Dark, Charlie Davis, Christine Pearson, Will Randle, Derek Toulalan, Steve Walker and Dave Webster. Particular thanks go to Brigitte Randle for her photographs and tolerance and to Ian Smith of *Perspective* and *High* magazine for his tireless efforts to get quality photographs for me, often in appalling conditions. Harold Drasdo, Harry Griffin and Richard Else have also been generous with their support, advice, knowledge and photographs for which, grateful thanks. David Craig and Terry Gifford have been consistently supportive. Without their cajoling, fruitful criticism of my writing and challenging companionship on the hill, I doubt whether this book would have been written.

My parents have provided rest and recuperation in Natland and a sympathetic ear when it has been needed most, and Graham and Sarah Chaplin-Bryce of Low Bridge End Farm in St John's in the Vale, always guaranteed me a warm and welcoming base from which to operate over the two years.

I wish to thank the editors of *Cumbria* and *High* magazines who published versions of three essays which appear in the book: 'Out of the Ark', 'Victorian Values' and 'Stonewalling'; and the President of the Fell and Rock Climbing Club for permission to quote from the journals of the club.

Finally, I wish to record my deepest gratitude and appreciation to my wife Sally for her support during difficult times. Her active involvement with all aspects of this book has guaranteed its completion.

John Baker climbs the crux of Eliminate A, watched by David Craig belayed from the rochers perchés *stance*

I·N·D·E·X